Richard Murphy: Poet of Two Traditions

Other works by Maurice Harmon

The Poetry of Thomas Kinsella: 'With darkness for a nest'. Wolfhound Press (Dublin, 1974). Humanities Press (New York, 1975).

Select Bibliography for the Study of Anglo-Irish Literature and its Backgrounds. Wolfhound Press (Dublin, 1977). P.D. Meany Co. Inc. Publishers (Port Credit, Canada, 1977)

A Literary Map of Ireland. Ed. Wolfhound Press (Dublin, 1977)

Richard Murphy:
Poet of Two Traditions

Interdisciplinary Studies

Edited by
Maurice Harmon

Wolfhound Press

ISBN 0 905473 17 5

Wolfhound Press
98 Ardilaun Portmarnock
County Dublin

Acknowledgements
The publisher acknowledges with thanks the *Irish
University Review: A Journal of Irish Studies* for
permission to include the text of its 'Special Issue'
(Vol. 7 No. 1 Spring 1977) on the poetry of Richard
Murphy in this edition.© *Irish University Review*. All
photographs, including cover, by Peter Johnson.

Contents

Note on the Contributors

Maurice Harmon: Editor of the *Irish University Review: a Journal of Irish Studies.* Teaches at University College, Dublin. **Seamus Heaney:** Irish poet. Teaches at Carysfort College of Education, Dublin. **Richard Murphy:** At present teaches at the University of Iowa. **J.G. Simms:** Teaches at Trinity College, Dublin. **Michael Herity:** President, Royal Society of Antiquaries of Ireland. Teaches at University College, Dublin.**Anthony Whilde:** Research Fellow with the Game Research Unit of the Agricultural Institute. **Jonathan Williams:** Publisher, Sugarloaf Press. Formerly with Institute of Public Administration, Dublin. Now publishing in Canada. **Mary FitzGerald:** Teaches at Fordham University, New York.

Editor's Preface

The Richard Murphy issue of the *Irish University Review*, which forms the substance of this book, was launched on the island of Inishbofin in April, 1977. Richard had come from America to be guest of honour at the island's Arts Festival and for his daughter's twenty-first birthday (Emily was born in Dublin on 19th May, 1956). When he gave a reading of his poems in the National School, the room was filled with those attending the festival and with people from the island itself. Seated in the front row was his old friend, Pat Concannon, to whom he dedicated the reading.

He read superbly, with a keen sense of occasion, with authority and skill, his voice carrying the rhythms of poems like "Sailing to an Island", "The Cleggan Disaster" and "Pat Cloherty's Version of *The Maisie*" with a flexibility of tone, cadence and resonance. He read only poems that had their origins in the life of the region and among its people. When some of them actually wept during his narration of "The Cleggan Disaster", their feelings seemed to confirm the validity and integrity of his relationship with them as man and poet.

That relationship has been a strong factor in his life and work, but Richard Murphy is a poet of two traditions. His deep attraction to the people of the western seaboard does not involve a denial of his own Ascendancy background. He aims to explore both the Irish and the Anglo-Irish traditions. To these he responds through a sense of history and of ancestry, with an awareness of place, and a feeling for event. The interpretation and evaluation of his poetry involves us in the kind of interdisciplinary task that has been undertaken in this book—in a poet-critic's placing of the poetry in the two traditions, in an historian's consideration of the Battle of Aughrim as interpreted by the historian and as treated by the poet, in an archaeologist's survey of the High Island sanctuary, in the notes on the birds, in the annotations on the long poems, in the bibliography, in the biographical notes. These, we hope, will be useful in future studies of the poet's work.

Maurice Harmon

Introduction: The Poet and His Background

> *The poetry of Sophocles is light shining through and*
> *piercing the darkness and making it plain and making*
> *it clear. That's something that appeals to me very much.*
> *It tends in a way towards poetry which is an accurate*
> *memory of the tribe, of the people: a way of preserving*
> *the truth about the past, rather than poetry as a magical*
> *incantation or ritual.*
>
> Richard Murphy

From the beginning of his poetic career Richard Murphy worked hard to achieve clarity; the struggle may be traced in the early uncollected pieces with their apocalyptic touches from Dylan Thomas, their austere notes from Milton and their Wordsworthian passion for nature, but it is central to his growth as a writer. He always seeks the exact word and the precise meaning, making it clear being more important than making it new. At the same time he is a formalist who favours traditional verse forms and standard metres.

One of his basic beliefs is the truth of place; he is drawn by the drama of what happened in a specific place—Wittgenstein at Rosroe, Roethke at Inishbofin. His accounts of journeys by sea are based on an actual voyage and an actual disaster. He sets poems in specific places, Brittany, Crete, Creragh, Cleggan, Aughrim, and because of its topographical density, his work has a strong regional dimension.

Another prominent characteristic, arising from his interest in place and event, is the attraction for narrative. He believes that there is truth in accurate historical narrative; he therefore takes great care to establish the reality of particular events, that certain things happened and exactly how. This fundamental need determines both his preparation for the writing of a particular poem and for the method of organisation. His narratives, "Sailing to an Island", "The Cleggan Disaster", and "The Last Galway Hooker", are constructed in such a way that their effectiveness is the result of the careful presentation of their narrative components, their accurate record of things done and said.

The value of these descriptive narratives is relative to their meaning for one mind. "The poet's mind", as Murphy once noted, "has become the stage on which the action takes place, and the myth is treated as an indication or reflection of that mind." That observation, made about the general decline in narrative poetry, is particularly relevant to *The Battle of Aughrim* which, for all its diversity, is a drama of a single consciousness. Murphy's aim is to strip away the myths that time, tradition and conflicting attitudes have imposed on the event, so that its truth can shine through the faithful, almost documentary, narrative.

His own assessment of what he was trying to do, couched in the language of logic and mathematics, allows us to understand his attitude to the poem and to see its principle of organisation:

> . . . I was trying to get clear a division in my mind between England and Ireland—between an almost entirely English education, an English mind and Irish feeling. I tried to reconcile these two by focussing on the battle (in which my ancestors fought on both sides), finding out all I could, what it was really about and what people thought it was about; putting in different points of view, the errors and atrocities of which myths are made, and drawing up an evaluation of what the religious conflict meant: what it meant in the past and how the past is still influencing us.

The world of Aughrim becomes a stage, a drama of contrasting voices, figures, events and 'sides', focussed by a presiding narrator: they are reflections from an individual mind determined to get the 'equation' right.

The key to much of Murphy's work comes from this need to bridge the gap between the two cultures and the two traditions, to achieve a balance between planted demesne and peasant holding, between what he sees as the isolation and rectitude of the one and the sense of community and freedom of the other. In some respects he seems to be a classic example of a sensibility divided between the two major traditions of Irish life, but the dichotomies that are visible in his work, indeed clarified there for our consideration, should not encourage us to see it merely as a stereotype of the Ascendancy-peasant relationship or to categorise it within a conventional view of that relationship based on a particular period, a particular region, or even its imaginative reconstruction by other poets. Murphy's definitions of ancestry and of self, and his sense of relationships between places and cultures, are peculiar to his own experience. There are many dimensions to his understanding of faded ancestry, poor gentry, plantation and rectory; there are, too, many facets to his vision of people of the other culture, those in between the two and those outside both. Aughrim itself he saw as the "navel", Ireland's geographical centre, and that physical fact confirmed his sense of it as a familial, religious, social, historical and cultural centre as well, from which virtually everything of importance radiates, including his own destiny. *The Battle of Aughrim* itself is a complex act of understanding, as though by working out the problem on the page he could then write Q.E.D. after it and move on to 'more personal poetry'.

The transition to *High Island*, with its three separate but complementary worlds, indicates the discovery of another centre, the preparation of another drama in which a variety of separate actions can be realised. The notes of love and imaginative possession, the liberation of language and feeling, the Hardyesque purity of diction suggest how fruitful this mating of self and landscape has been.

The integrity of Richard Murphy's poetic career is apparent in the successive acts of definition and scrutiny that make up the bulk of his work. As a young man he set sail for an island of vision, but found instead the inner harbour at Inishbofin and men in the real world. Ever since, he has trusted reality and meets it on its own terms. Today his chosen landscape is full of potential for myth or magical incantation, but his manner is still low-keyed and objective. The stormpetrel is his pulse of the rock, her nest a hermit's skull; it is the thrift and sea-campion that flower, the pink granite of St Fechin's church that rises from the dead, aided by the skill of the archaeologists, the cross-slab at Brian Boru's well that retains its power for a thousand years. The corncrake drafts an epic, the petrels compose a nocturne. To these he bears witness in his poetry, to these creatures, these harmonies, these movements and events in the natural and the real world.

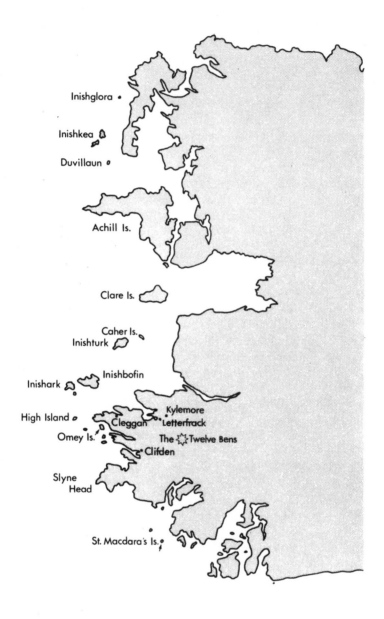

The Coast of Counties Galway and Mayo

Maurice Harmon

Biographical Note on Richard Murphy

1927 (6 August) Born at Milford House, County Galway, third child of William Lindsay Murphy and Elizabeth Mary Ormsby. Taken to Ceylon.

1929–31 Back in Ireland; lives beside Lough Corrib, not far from his grandfather's rectory at Oughterard.

1932–35 Returns to Ceylon; for the first eight years of his life has a British nanny, Mrs Maud Wallis.

1932–37, his father is Chairman of the Municipal Council and Mayor of Colombo.

In 1934 Richard is relieved to get away from the strange and exotic world of Ceylon; he visits the Holy Land on the return voyage.

1935–37 Lives at Rosleague House, near Letterfrack, Connemara; goes to Kylemore Abbey School for six months. An enjoyable period of his life.

(September) Goes to Baymount Preparatory School, Dollymount, Dublin, a Protestant boarding school; is taught by a brilliant mathematics teacher, Sidney Patterson. The boys play war games in the school yard.

1937–40 Wins a voice trial for the Canterbury Cathedral Choir. Sees the Imperial War Museum in London: his first contact with the mythology of World War I. Sees the place where Charles I, one of his ancestors through an illegitimate line, was beheaded. At his school in Canterbury, the emphasis is on music; he studies harmony and composition, composing anthems and magnificats in the style of Charles Villiers Stanford. As a boy soprano he sings Purcell, Palestrina and the whole range of church music; becomes a senior chorister in 1940; wants to be a composer. Enjoys Canterbury very much as a historical city and likes the school. The outbreak of World War II disturbs this life: the boys are evacuated to Cornwall; then Richard is brought back to Milford House after the fall of Dunkirk.

1940–41 A blissful period on the beautiful Cromwellian demesne. The children have private tutors: Sally Stokes, an intellectual disciplinarian, who had been a playmate of C.S. Lewis's in Belfast; she changes Richard's interest from music

11

to poetry, to Milton, Wordsworth and Eliot. The other tutor, a Classicist who looks like a Viking, is Thomas Thackaberry; he had taught in many of Ireland's public schools.

1941   Wins a Milner scholarship to King's School, Canterbury. The school had been moved to Carlyon Bay Hotel, St Anstall, in Wales; spends four terms there.

1943–45   (January)   Goes to Wellington College, Berkshire, a school with military traditions, where he has Raymond Carr and T.S. Dorsch as teachers. The army played an important part in his family: his elder brother joined the Royal Ulster Rifles; his father's brother was killed in World War I; on his mother's side there was a long tradition of distinguished army careers, stretching through the Boer, Napoleonic and Peninsular Wars. To die for religion and country was one of the strongest sentiments in his upbringing; as a boy he had daydreams about battles. Now, at Wellington, he revolts against the system, becomes a pacifist, something of a loner, and an intellectual, and begins to write poetry.

1944–48   Wins a Demyship to Magdalen College, Oxford, attracted by C.S. Lewis who had been Dorsch's tutor. His tutor for Anglo-Saxon is J.A.W. Bennett.

1946   Rents his first cottage in Connemara, on Lough Fee. Works on a verse play about Lynch of Galway who hanged his own son; it is a Jacobean melodrama on the theme of justice, in which he contrasts Irish and English concepts of law and punishment.   Leaves Oxford; seeks peace in Connemara; his grandmother persuades him to return.

1948   Graduates with a good Second in English Language and Literature. Goes to the Bahamas in August to act as aide-de-camp to his father who is in his last year as Governor.

1949   To make money to go back to Connemara, takes a job with an insurance brokers attached to Lloyds.   Lives with his sister Mary in very poor circumstances in Fulham; walks around areas of the city associated with *The Waste Land*. Reviews for *The Spectator* and *The Times Literary Supplement*.

1951   Wins AE award (£100). Goes to Connemara for two years; rents Quay House in Rosroe where Wittgenstein had lived in 1949; finds some of the philosopher's letters in the turf shed. The land had once belonged to his great-grandfather, General Thomson of Salruck House. He is very poor. Writes "My Three and Twentieth Year" and "Snow" in the Lough Fee cottage.

1952   (April–September)   Has a job as night watchman on the Erriff River, guarding against poachers.

Wants to bring together the two sides of his experience, the trained intelligence and critical faculty of his English education and the more emotional, more earthy Irish side. Writes an epic about Diarmuid and Grainne; changes the theme to one of flight from the City, from London, to the isolation of the West. D.H. Lawrence's story "The Man Who Loved Islands" indicates the direction his life was taking.

(Summer) He and his brother try to sail to Clare Island but are driven, nine hours later, to Inishbofin. The *Bell* version of "Sailing to an Island" comes out of this.

Is paid £6 for poems in *The Bell*; able to go to London.

Renews his reviewing for *The Spectator* and *The Times Literary Supplement*.

1953 (January—March) Does some tutoring at the Davies Lang and Dick school.

(Summer) Returns to Rosroe.

(September) Goes to Crete as Director of the English School in Canea. Lives in the village of Agios Matthaios; gives some private lessons.

1954 (Summer) Returns to Ireland.

(Autumn) Takes a course on French civilisation at the Sorbonne; studies Racine and Stendhal. Meets Patricia Avis, his future wife, a fellow-student at the Sorbonne; writes his Paris poems.

He and Patricia go to Brittany where he writes "Girl at the Seaside" and "Auction".

1955 They go to Greece and to Crete in the Spring; he writes "To a Cretan Monk" and "The Archaeology of Love". The former was written at Phaestos in a guest-house overlooking a valley that fed Roman legionaries in the Minoan period; the harvester's vase came from Ayia Triadha, nearby.

(May) Marries Patricia Avis; she had contributed poems to *The Listener* and *Poetry Now* and had taken a medical degree at Oxford. They return to Rosroe, with an Old English sheep-dog called 'Rocky-Face', a gift from Richard to his wife. He prepares a collection of poems of his choice for the BBC, including some previously unpublished work by Philip Larkin, Theodore Roethke and Valentin Iremonger.

1956 (19 May) Birth in Dublin of their daughter, Emily.

1956—57 The Murphys buy 'Lake Park', an attractive regency lodge on Lough Dan, County Wicklow, from Ernest Gebler and Edna O'Brien. They rebuild the house, reclaim the two hundred acres, reseed them with deep-rooting herbs, and fence and stock the property with Wicklow Mountain Cheviot Sheep.

Tragedy intrudes upon this happy period, with the death of Patricia's sister-in-law and the sudden death some months later of her brother, Cesje. The Murphys invite the two children to stay with them and enlarge the house; it is Richard's first building job, working with direct labour.

The Murphys move to London and are divorced the following year.

1958 (Autumn) Buys a house in London; he lectures at Morley College and gives extra-mural lectures at London University. His grandmother, Lucy Mary Ormsby, dies in January; she is buried in Kilmaine, County Mayo, from the church in which Richard had been christened. He is already working on the poem about her, "The Woman of the House".

1959 "The Woman of the House" is broadcast on the Third Programme, produced by George MacBeth; published in an edition of 250 copies by Dolmen Press, Dublin. A lengthy discussion ensues in *The Times Literary Supplement* and elsewhere.

(June) Goes to Inishbofin, where he meets Tony White; they become close friends. Renews his friendship with Pat Concannon; goes fishing with him in his *pookhaun*. Decides to buy a boat. "The Cleggan Disaster" begins to take shape. Seeks an active life to counteract his sense of failure after the dissolution of his marriage. Buys the *Ave Maria* from Michael Schofield, P.C., of Inishbofin; he and Tony White clear out the hold.

1959–60 Teaches again at Morley College; stays with his parents in Rhodesia for three months. From this visit comes "The God Who Eats Corn". Writes the first fifteen or twenty lines of "The Last Galway Hooker", finishing it on Inishbofin on Shrove Tuesday 1960.

(17 March) Makes first voyage in the *Ave Maria*, with Pat Cloherty of the *Maisie* and his brother-in-law, Pat Concannon. Aspires to sail around the world; loves the literature of the sea —Melville, Slocum, Dana. Runs a business on the *Ave Maria*, bringing tourists on trips and lobster fishing.

(Summer) Visit to Inishbofin by Theodore Roethke and his wife.

1960 (Autumn and Winter) Moves to 11 Upper Mount Street, Dublin, where he writes "The Poet on the Island", the final version of "Sailing to an Island" and the first part of "The Cleggan Disaster".

Takes part in a poetry reading at the Hibernian Hotel, Dublin

14

with John Montague and Thomas Kinsella.

1961 (Spring) "The Last Galway Hooker" published in *The Listener*. Returns to Cleggan: advertises his boating business; begins a physically demanding period in which he gives all his energy to making a success of his work with the *Ave Maria*. Buys a cottage in Cleggan; gives up his fantasy of sailing round the world. Buys *The Truelight* from Martin Oliver in the Claddagh, Galway; she was the next to last hooker built there. The boatwright was John Rainey; Pat Cloherty built the *Ave Maria* on Long Walk, behind the Spanish Arch in Galway. Sails *The Truelight* from Galway, round Slyne Head, taking twenty hours to reach Cleggan; refits her in Inishbofin and takes on John O'Halloran to sail her. Cleggan begins to thrive on the business generated by the two hookers. His work is encouraged and aided by Matthew and Eileen O'Malley of the Pier Bar in Cleggan. Finishes "The Cleggan Disaster" in his cottage at Cleggan; his own night voyage from Spiddal to Cleggan with Owen Coyne helps him to imagine the night journey in the Cleggan disaster. Reads the poem to Pat Concannon, who says "What you've said is true. And it's well put together."

1962 (January) Submits a collection of poems, *Sailing to an Island*, to Faber and Faber; while waiting for their decision adds "The Travelling Player" and "The Drowning of a Novice". "The Cleggan Disaster" is published in *The Dolmen Miscellany*; accepted also by Douglas Cleverdon for the BBC; read by Denys Hawthorne.

Wins first prize of £75 in the Guinness Poetry Award at Cheltenham for "Years Later", the epilogue to "The Cleggan Disaster". The poem is printed in the Handbook of the Cheltenham Festival of Literature.

Sylvia Plath and Ted Hughes visit at Cleggan; she is much taken by the sea. They visit Coole Park and Ballylee. Richard has just started work on *The Battle of Aughrim*; thinks of it as a descriptive narrative poem. Ted Hughes recommends dramatic monologues. Richard enjoys Sylvia Plath's conversation and personality and writes some of the best parts of *The Battle of Aughrim* under that stimulus.

(Autumn) Reviews for *The Observer*.

1963 (January) Is in London; contributes "The Pleasure Ground" to BBC series.

(January) Faber publish *Sailing to an Island*; it goes through three hardback impressions, then into paperback. Sees Sylvia Plath for the last time; is deeply upset by her death. Decides to discontinue his boating business.

(Summer and Autumn) Writes "The God Who Eats Corn", commissioned by Leonard Russell of *The Sunday Times*.

1964 Publication of the poem, planned for 4 January to coincide with the demise of the Central African Federation, is changed because of the Pope's visit to the Holy Land.

(October–November) Poetry reading tour in America. Sells *The Truelight*. Does little sailing after 1964; decides to give up his London flat.

1965 (Summer) Goes to America.

Works on *The Battle of Aughrim*; stays in Aughrim with Martin Joyce and gathers information about the battle and its lore. On another visit rides about the battlefield on horseback.

(August–September) Begins to build a house in Cleggan.

(Autumn) Writer-in-residence at the University of Virginia.

(Winter) Ted Hughes and Assia Guttman live in Connemara. On 15 April of this year his father dies.

1966 (January–February) He and Ted Hughes meet regularly; Hughes beginning to work on the Crow poems.

(Summer) Richard is painfully ill with a virus infection of the mouth; spends two weeks in the Galway Regional Hospital. Tony White drives to Galway each day to see him; moves into the house and does the carpentry and painting.

(Christmas) Goes to Headfort, County Mayo to buy a caravan from a family of travellers; sees for the first time, under winter conditions, the life of the itinerants. Brings one child to live with him at Cleggan; teaches him to read and write. In the summer the boy runs off to the roads again.

1967 Finishes *The Battle of Aughrim*. Wins an Arts Council of Britain award; with the money buys a house for the family of travellers. Tries to teach another brother to read and write.

1968 The BBC broadcast *The Battle of Aughrim*; Faber publish it and "The God Who Eats Corn".

(Spring) Visiting lecturer at Reading University.

(Summer) Returns to Cleggan.

(Autumn) Is Compton Lecturer in Poetry at the University of Hull.

1969 (Spring) Buys High Island from Graham Tulloch; finds a carved stone there.

(Summer) Cleans Brian Boru's well and brings over two masons to make a horseshoe wall around it. Had taken his parents to the island in 1964; his father had been there as a boy with Dr Leeper, Richard's godfather and great-uncle by marriage.

1969–70 Begins to stay overnight on the island. Spends all of 1970 in Cleggan, visiting the island in the summer.

1971 (January) Goes to Colgate University, New York, as the Visiting O'Connor Professor of Literature.

(March) Goes on a poetry reading tour with Ted Hughes.

(Summer) Renovates one room of the miner's cottage on High Island. Writes "The Reading Lesson" and "Double Negative". The cottage becomes a place of retreat where he stays and works.

(Autumn) Returns to Colgate.

1972 (Spring) Writes "Seals at High Island" at Colgate; writes "Firebug", the first Ceylon poem.

(Autumn) Teaches at Bard College, New York.

(Summer) Spends several days at a time on High Island.

(May) Hears of two itinerant boys who have been committed to an industrial school; their five sisters have been committed to an orphanage in Dublin. Meets the parents who want the children back.

1973 (March) All the children are released to the parents on the understanding that Richard will help to rear them. He accepts responsibility for the whole family; gets them a house in Cleggan.

(Spring) Invited by the Abbey Theatre to be literary adviser for a production by Michael Cacoyannis of Yeats's version of Sophocles' *King Oedipus*.

(Autumn) Finishes the *High Island* collection.

1974 (February) Goes to Bard College.

(Summer) Returns to Cleggan; builds the hexagon on Omey Island.

(Autumn) Visiting poet at Princeton University.

1975 (Spring) Back at Princeton; writes long article on Philip Larkin for *The New York Review of Books*.

1976 (January) Deeply grieved by the sudden death of Tony White.

Wins British Arts Council Award.

(Spring) Invited to Yeats Festival at the State University of New York at Stonybrook.

1976–77 Teaches in the Writers Workshop at the University of Iowa.

Seamus Heaney

The Poetry of Richard Murphy

As a poet, Richard Murphy has something in common with the Orcadian poet George Mackay Brown. Both write about islands redolent of old faiths and old customs, about fishermen and tinkers, about landscapes and seascapes. Both manage a language that is objective and concrete, shaped and sided, closer to the staccato and stress of Anglo-Saxon poetry than to the melody and syntactical complexity of the Spenserean tradition. Both tend to keep themselves out of the poem, to be present as observers, anonymous voices, bearers of tales; they strike us as shapers of material rather than explorers of the self. Yet in spite of the facility with which the case for similarity can be made, it is the differences between them that are most significant.

Mackay Brown's style holds the actual world in thrall; his artistic world constitutes a frieze, an illuminated book of cold northern hours; the beauty of the art stands against the mess of the actual, its timeless images and archetypes, its corn and wine and waves and furrows are sacramental, cyclic alternatives to the profanity, vulgarity and decay he sees in contemporary life. The poetry is held like a cross in the face of the devilish onset of a deracinated materialism, an impious rationalism. It is a sign made in the name of an older, almost medieval consciousness, and its stiffness is the stiffness of ritual gesture.

Murphy's stiffness, on the other hand, is that of a man moving in a constricted space. The elemental characters and incidents in his work are not frozen in a heraldic procession but are in motion behind the pane of the style, where they are observed not with votive attachment but with precise detachment. They represent neither an exemplary nor an alternative world but are rendered as aspects of the world we inhabit and, if the epic note is occasionally sounded above them, they maintain a documentary presence that almost shrugs off heroism. Whereas Mackay Brown offers his world as the emblem of a desirable culture to which he would be affiliated, Murphy conducts us into a bleak and beautiful environment toward which he is sympathetic but finally ambivalent. Murphy's fidelity to the world of boatmen and tinkers and natural beauties and disasters does not altogether constitute a faith in it

18

because that world is inadequate to his social and cultural recognitions. It is valid in so far as the poet participates in it as boatman, as neighbour, as eavesdropper, as annalist, but it is unsatisfactory because this participation can never be total. Murphy will not surrender his sense of caste, his manners, his educated consciousness, his willed individuality to this essentially communal fatalistic and half-literate culture, however attractively that culture presents itself to his imagination. The constricted space he moves in and writes out of is a march between his Anglo-Irish Protestant background and his Irish Catholic surroundings, a space at once as neutral and torn as the battlefield at Aughrim, as problematic and personal as the house he builds for himself from ruined famine cottages, sometimes invaded by nostalgia for the imperial, patrician past, sometimes hospitable to deprivations and disasters which somehow rebuke that heritage.

* * *

The title poem of his first collection, *Sailing to an Island*, discovers that space in the shape of a narrow bed, a point of rest attained after some bruising of the social self. The poem is at once a direct narrative about a boat trip, full of the swing and threat of the sea, confident in its relish of sailing lingo, rich in evocation of atmospheres; and at the same time it is a parable of another journey between cultures, from the sure ground of a shared but disappearing Ascendancy world to the suspecting community of the native islanders. Although the boat runs into and negotiates a storm (and there is something Conradian about this test of seamanship), the real test is to survive the scrutiny of these secretive, knowing spectators:

What will the islanders think of our folly?

The whispering spontaneous reception committee
Nods and smokes by the calm jetty.
Am I jealous of these courteous fishermen
Who hand us ashore, for knowing the sea
Intimately, for respecting the storm
That took nine of their men on one bad night . . . ?

The answer is finally very Irish—well, yes, and no. Jealous, yes, of the sea-mysteries they possess, but finally content to hold to one's ability to set one's own course:

I slip outside, fall among stones and nettles,
Crackling dry twigs on an elder tree,

. . . .

Later, I reach a room, where the moon stares
Cobwebbed through the window. The tide has ebbed,
Boats are careened in the harbour. Here is a bed.

That bed is a point of rest but by no means a point of relapse or repose. There is a strong sense that tomorrow will renew the exposure, the search for balance, the need for skilled navigation. But the poem itself is secure in its art, a beautifully modulated movement from delight to wisdom; it achieves a momentary stay against confusion and by its honest plotting of a rite of passage earns its right to pass. Of course, the felicities of image and expression enrich our response ("the shelved Atlantic groundswell/ Plumbed by the sun's kingfisher rod"), although a too literary straining sometimes disturbs it ("the ribald face of a mad mistress"); but the poem's strength resides in the mythic and psychological truths exhaled off its plot. The narrative element is the adequate symbol.

In his suggestive essay, "The Pleasure Ground", (printed in 1964 in the BBC publication, *Writers on Themselves*), Murphy makes an imaginative connection between his childhood entrancement in the overgrown thickets of a pleasure ground and his later discovery of the sea as the first element in which his poetry came to life. The pleasure ground was a walled Ascendancy garden attached to his grandfather's house in the west of Ireland. It had run wild, but under the untutored profusion of yews, laurels and briars there lingered the ordered lines of ancestral care. When he arrived there as a boy with his mother, brother and sister, they made an effort to restore its decorous features, and the delight that came from this adventure of entering and ordering such natural abundance, he tells us, pervaded the disciplines of his education: his study of mathematics, music, painting and poetry was enlivened by the spirit of the garden. The essay ends with this tantalising sentence:

As I grew older the garden grew wilder, losing its form as trees were felled, and its spirit as old people died and the young left the country; so I searched more and more into the origins of that garden till I found them finally in the sea.

What does he mean? How does he find the origins of that garden in the sea? The answer to the question must be fundamental to the groundplan of Murphy's poetic imagination.

The garden went to wrack and ruin because of an absence of the shaping spirit. When his grandmother was finally left in charge of the place, she became "the mistress of a beautiful disorder". "There was no masculine energy in the place, to mend walls, plant new trees, sow and cultivate and labour. I felt lost, and guilty." That guilt is best understood in the light of Yeats's meditation on "Ancestral Houses":

And maybe the great-grandson of that house . . .

It is as if the young Murphy were unconsciously wincing under that taunt. But then the greatness of the ancestral order was founded upon violence. The estate had been in the family since the victories of William of Orange. "The planters of our pleasure ground had acquired an estate of 70,000 acres which famine, revolution and liberalism had cut down to its present size of 300 acres." This debilitation of the Protestant nation, which Yeats attempted to transcend and mystify by a magnificent transfusion of renaissance and eighteenth-century energies, Murphy is, however, ready to accept. Where Yeats was tyrannical and obstinate, continuously masculine in his promulgation of an archaic order, playing Canute to the modern tide, Murphy, sympathetic to the tender feminine concessions of his grand-mother, is prepared to swim that tide—not altogether with it, indeed, but at least at an angle to it that acknowledges its currents the better to ride them.

His grandmother came from the Atlantic coast and introduced the children to the Connemara landscape and its inhabitants, and these visits in her company renewed in the future poet an intimacy with the sea and the hills which he had experienced there during short periods in his early childhood, when this maritime wilderness had been his original pleasure ground. This new encounter with the Connemara ethos was more conscious, however:

These people lived on five or only two-and-a-half acre holdings, and we loved them better than our own relations, or the children at the rectory parties we had to attend. They were truly Irish and that's what my brother and I wanted to be . . . Stones, salmon-falls, rain clouds and drownings had entered and shaped their minds, loaded with ancestral bias. Their manners seemed more natural than ours, and their singing voices rasped excitingly against the hymn-tune harmonies we were used to. We wished we could talk like them.

To wish you could talk like somebody else is to seek to begin again with a new identity. It seems to me that Murphy exchanged the stewardship of his inherited pleasure ground for the stewardship of his chosen art; his "masculine energy" was directed to the mastery of a way of life among boats that would make him an initiate among the "truly Irish", and directed also to the mastery of the craft of poetry that would enable the rebirth of the self as an artist. As artist, he is impersonal and in control. The contents of his mind, the drift of his feelings, the conflict of his loyalties and recognitions are all materials to be worked, and the poem will have to be a vessel sturdy enough to take the strain of conflicting Irish winds. As Irish artist, both the pleasure ground of the elemental landscape, with its indigenous inhabitants, and the pleasure ground of the ancestral estate, with its colonial ethos, are to be his theme. He will fulfil the paternalistic role of his Governor father and the life-enhancing role of his grandmother by celebrating the noblest aspects of both cultures and perpetuating their purest strengths and values in his work. We might say that the sense of a rest well deserved, which informs the conclusion of "Sailing to an Island", is born from a realisation that perfection of the life has at least guaranteed perfection of that work.

"The Pleasure Ground" was published a year after the appearance of *Sailing to an Island* and stands as a coda to that book, as well as a prologue to *The Battle of Aughrim*. Indeed, although I have forced the essay to stand as a gloss on the title poem of the first collection, it is much more explicitly relevant to the other three long poems in the book, "The Last Galway Hooker", "The Cleggan Disaster" and "The Woman of the House". Each of these is severely formal. The first thing we respond to is the finish of the verse, the eccentric stress of the metric, the conscious wording. This is clinker-built poetry and, unless it is buoyant upon deep feeling or strong sensation, it feels cumbersome. For this reason, while I can take pleasure in the poet's pleasure in his last Galway hooker, I feel that that poem's prose sense and mass sink its poetic lift. It is is if we have been provided with a barge where a currach might have been more appropriate. Nevertheless, its theme of inheritance and renewal is central to the volume; more explicit than "Sailing to an Island", though not, I think, as artistically successful, it celebrates the furbishing of a boat and a betrothal to its mysteries as analogous to the poet's artistic commitment to making, continuing and conserving.

"The Woman of the House" is a grave and tender elegy to that "mistress of a beautiful disorder" whose memory "warms my mind". Beneficent, munificent, she is made to walk again behind the dry-stone walls of the quatrains, each of which forms a kind of invocation:

> She fed our feelings as dew feeds the grass
> On April nights, and our mornings were green:

She is almost a muse, and that echo of a medieval carol to the Virgin Mary is entirely appropriate to our sense of her as a nurturing presence, as a mother of perpetual succour, an intermediary between the extra-mural world of labourers' cottages and patrician evenings with biscuits on a tray and ginger wine. *Gravitas, pietas*—elevating classical notions present themselves when we look for the quick of the poem's feelings. Yet there is a resolute matter-of-factness that does not balk at her certified dotage and gives a hard force to the last snatch of her talk:

> 'They left me in this gaol. You all tell lies.
> You're not my people. My people have gone.'

It is unlikely, of course, that "her people" would have called her "the woman of the house". The phrase is a translation of the Irish *bean a'tighe*, so that the poem's title stands in that narrow march between two languages and two traditions which Lucy Mary Ormsby sought to establish in her life and which the poet seeks to occupy in his art.

The intonations of "The Woman of the House" are drawn from the world of phaetons and sermons; the tact and reticence of the opening stanza bow slightly from the waist:

> On a patrician evening in Ireland
> I was born in the guest-room: she delivered me.
> May I deliver her from the cold hand
> Where now she lies, with a brief elegy?

The opening of "The Cleggan Disaster", on the other hand, bows to the labour of rowing, and is loaded with a different "ancestral bias":

Five boats were shooting their nets in the bay
After dark. It was cold and late October.
The hulls hissed and rolled on the sea's black hearth
In the shadow of stacks close to the island.
Rain drenched the rowers, with no drying wind .

The feeling for the sea in this work is very different from Synge's in *Riders to the Sea*. There is no real merging into the fisherman's point of view, no unbending of the authorial voice, no tinge of the *keen*, no surrender to the intimate vocabulary of the fishermen. Instead, there is that strong "masculine energy", a robust framing of the scene, a narrative pace that takes things almost with a tradesman's calm and thoroughness. The result is a beautifully solid, slow and stoic presentation of the disaster. If it misses the *duende* that Synge achieves, it registers authoritatively the *sensation* of the sea's relentless and awesome power. I used to think that the loving art bestowed on the texture of the thing impeded the story, that the poet was needlessly working a tapestry, where what was required was something more like a newsreel, but my sense of the poem has changed. The kind of thing I was imagining has been done since, in fact, by Murphy, in "Pat Cloherty's Version of *The Maisie*" (in *High Island*) but when we compare this work with the earlier poem, we realise that the loaded, encrusted, stained-glass richness of "The Cleggan Disaster" serves, in Yeats's words, "to prolong the moment of contemplation", and that Murphy's gift is not for the dramatic but for the picturesque—in the sense that "The Eve of St Agnes" is picturesque. What we are given is a *via dolorosa* of the waves, and the achievement of its objective bulk must have encouraged the poet to face the larger disaster that happened at Aughrim in 1691.

* * *

The Battle of Aughrim is as meditative as it is narrative, in so far as the juxtaposition of the historical elements induces a detached consideration of the meaning of the action (or is it actions?) now, before, during and after the battle. The story-telling voice shifts its perspectives and varies its intonations to enliven different parts of the tale, but its function is finally choric, setting things in an ironic and tragic pattern. Two details from the poem give us some idea of its time-span: near the beginning a pious and resentful Catholic woman brings the poet a souvenir from Knock shrine, "John Kennedy's head on a china dish"; near the end, a party of

French visitors, descendants of the Wild Geese, tour the battlefield and remember "Seed, there should be seed, buried in a cairn." Both images have the effect of suggesting a continuing mythic or metaphoric order in things, yet keep close to the literal and the actual, so that while we are invited to intuit some hermetic link between the beheading of St Ruth and the head of the murdered Kennedy, between primeval deposits in the ground associating growth with burial and the visitation of the battlefield by descendants of its losers, we are left to make what we can of these facts. The poet, in Patrick Kavanagh's words, merely states the position, trying to imagine "Exactly what took place, what it could mean,/Whether by will or by chance".

Yet the poem is fundamentally connected with Murphy's shaping of his inheritance into a poetic theme: his quarrel with himself is implicit in the lines of the battle, and the violence within modern Ireland "Has a beginning in my blood." He can trace affiliations with both sides. Patrick Sarsfield, Earl of Lucan, darling of the defeated Irish side, is plangently celebrated as "great-uncle in the portrait's grime" and the buoyancy and melody of this section of the poem touch racial stops that the Reverend George Story, author of *An Impartial History of the Wars in Ireland*, would surely find regrettable:

> At Limerick besieged, you led the dance:
> 'If this had failed, I would have gone to France.'
> When youths lit brandy in a pewter dish
> You were their hazel nut and speckled fish.

On the other hand, feelings not unexpected from the author of "The Pleasure Ground" are raised in a lyric that celebrates the colonist's vision and forges incidentally a thematic link between the title poem and "The God Who Eats Corn", also included in this volume:

> 'Slow sigh of the garden yews
> Forty years planted.
> May the God of battle
> Give us this day our land
> And the papists be trampled.
> . . . .
> I am loyal to fields I have sown
> And the king reason elected:
> Not to a wine-blotted birth-mark

Of prophecy, but hard work
Deepening the soil for seed.'

And in the "Now" section, the poet is affronted by a
"kinsman"—and how tactfully his use of that proud noun places
him at a distance from the man himself and from the less dynastic
consciousness of the "truly Irish"—who violates both the
indigenous and the colonial heritages:

Left a Cromwellian demesne
My kinsman has bulldozed three bronze age raths.
. . . .
He's auctioned grandfather's Gallipoli sword
And bought a milking machine.

It is by such means that Murphy seeks to pattern conflicting
facts and facets of history and Irishry. The whole poem is a
tessellation of deliberately shaped lyrics, just in their long views,
solid in their crafted shapes, occasionally rich in their violent
content—as in the account of the death of the traitor Luttrell—
or entranced by the satisfactions of their language, as in the
evocation of rapparees who materialise before the battle "Out of
the earth, out of the air, out of the water". Yet in this lovely
section there is a symptomatic unease between the manner and
the matter of the poetry:

. . . At the whirr of a snipe each can disappear

Terrified as a bird in a gorse-bush fire,
To delve like a mole or mingle like a nightjar
Into the earth, into the air, into the water.

Moles are not to be found in Ireland and nightjars have to my ear
an indelibly English literary ring to them, so that at a moment
when the tutelar presences of the Irish ground are being
summoned, they are subtly debilitated by the idiom in which they
surface. It is not that Murphy wishes to rob them of their proper
force: it is more that his language retains *its* ancestral bias in spite
of his intention to exorcise ancestry as a determining limit of
vision.

Mention of the poet's intention brings us to the critical crux. I
agree with Edna Longley[1] that "something programmatic in its
design and designs . . . stands in the way of total subjection of the

1. "Searching the Darkness" in Douglas Dunn (ed.), *Two Decades of Irish Writing*
(Cheadle Hulme: Carcanet Press, 1975), p. 130.

offered experience" and I am tempted to formulate my sense of what is missing, perhaps too glibly, in words from Robert Frost's "The Gift Outright", also a poem about the relationship of self to historical and geographical continuities:

Something we were witholding made us weak
Until we found out that it was ourselves
We were witholding from our land of living,
And forthwith found salvation in surrender.

It is as if in his first two volumes Murphy is intent on discovering navigational aids to locate the self, to plot its longitude and latitude. These books are the log of an expedition before they are the diary of a soul. In *High Island*, however, we enter more subjective territory and the intimacy of exploration, which Murphy showed himself capable of in his earlier poems about Theodore Roethke and Ludwig Wittgenstein ("The Poet on the Island" and "The Philosopher and the Birds"), is exercised upon the poet's own life. Solitude and ambivalence, love and loss, become explicitly personal themes. A freeing of the voice occurs and a number of poems combine a lightness of touch and an intensity of feeling that come from a quick surgery of these more intimate veins.

In Murphy's verse, we often sense the strain of the poem achieving itself line by line. When I mentioned Anglo-Saxon verse at the beginning, I was alluding, among other things, to this feeling of the mass of the poem being built from self-contained units; we are confronted with a worked-upon body of sense, a not unobtrusive metric, a balanced pillar of neatly dressed individual pieces. Consider this short section from *The Battle of Aughrim*:

'Teigue in his green coat rides to war,
Nuts are swelling in the hazel-wood.
My father's ten black heifers low,
I've lost the father of my unborn child.

Last night he left me in a copse to weep
When foragers bugled there'd be a battle.
Proudly he gallops in Sarsfield's troop,
My tongue less to him than a drum's rattle.'

The situation is that of the ruined maid in the greenwood. Each line is a self-contained unit, almost a gnomic utterance. There is

27

a richness of suggestion in the swelling nuts, the lowing heifers, even the green coat and the father/father play in lines 3 and 4. But there is also something conventional about the whole conception and an externality about the rhyme battle/rattle that is symptomatic of a lack of sympathetic imagining. The piece is picturesque in the bad sense, set into the structure of the long poem because it illustrates one of the consequences of the war, made up from the outside rather than discovered from the inside, deficient in a living rhythm. If we compare it with the conclusion of "Sunup" in *High Island*, also a poem about loss, we see how a vivid rhythm intensifies the greenwood imagery, and how the voice has been freed in its movement:

> Do you feel like this when you make love?
> Do you love her as I loved you?
> Will you let her steal all you have
> And suffer her to leave?
>
> Meet me today! We'll find a wood
> Of blackthorn in white bud:
> And let me give you one more kiss
> Full of sun, free of bitterness.

In *High Island* the old preoccupations are more internalised. Small incidents take large strains. We are aware of a sureness of direction in the art and a poised and appeased self-knowledge in the poet. "Walking on Sunday", for example, has the poise of self-possession about it, and a fluency and delight in its own music —a not unhappy music of time and change:

> Walking on Sunday into Omey Island
> When the tide had fallen slack,
> I crossed a spit of wet ribbed sand
> With a cold breeze at my back.
> . . . .
> Blood was returning dimly to the face
> Of the chancel they'd uncovered,
> Granite skin that rain would kiss
> Until the body flowered.

In "Little Hunger" the renewal that the archaeological uncovering achieves on Omey is matched by a renewal which the poet himself achieves when he builds a house from ruined cottages and repeats the old pattern of confiscation. There is a fine balance between self-reproach and self-justification in the last stanza, between the ruthless "dismemberment" and the restorative "integral":

> Once mine, I'd work on their dismemberment,
>   Threshold, lintle, wall;
> And pick a hearthstone from a rubble fragment
>   To make it integral.

Walking or driving or watching or listening, the poet in this volume is typically alone and in the best poems his encounters are translated into states of feeling. The most resonant of these is "Seals at High Island", evocative of place, analytical of feelings, replete with a music of sea and sex and sorrow, moving like a long swell, finding at last a syntax that carries over from line to line so that the effort of making is subsumed into the pleasures of saying:

> At nightfall they haul out, and mourn the drowned,
> Playing to the sea sadly their last quartet,
> An improvised requiem that ravishes
> Reason, while ripping scale up like a net:
> Brings pity trembling down the rocky spine
> Of headlands, till the bitter ocean's tongue
> Swells in their cove, and smothers their sweet song.

When read alongside the poems I have mentioned, the uptight bitter anecdotes about clifftop murder, caravan incest and quayside gossip and craft are too cold. On the other hand, the autobiographical childhood pieces about Ceylon are almost over-voluptuous: a wealth of tropical detail luxuriates around the line of the narrative and an unexpected exotic quality enters the poetry. A new pleasure ground, a new myth for what the poetry means, swims into his ken. Sound and self, not social and historical circumstances, are apprehended as the essentials. "Coppersmith" finds Murphy in the act of remaking his poetic myth, coming in close to the heart of the feeling, relaxing out happily in the run of the sense and the syntax. It begins in a narrow space but opens generously to concern itself not with the English colonial past but with the poetic resources of the English language, that medium where all of us, "truly Irish" or "Anglo-Irish", must discover ourselves and our directions, the bounds of our outer and our inner space:

A temple tree grew in our garden in Ceylon.
We knew it by no other name.
The flower, if you turned it upside down,
Looked like a dagoba with an onion dome.
A holy perfume
Stronger than the evil tang of betel-nut
Enticed me into its shade on the stuffiest afternoon,

Where I stood and listened to the tiny hammer-stroke
Of the crimson coppersmith perched above my head,
His *took took took*
And his *tonk tonk tonk*
Were spoken in a language I never understood:
And there I began to repeat
Out loud to myself an English word such as *beat beat beat*,

Till hammering too hard I lost the meaning in the sound
Which faded and left nothing behind,
A blank mind,
The compound spinning round,
My brain melting, as if I'd stood in the sun
Too long without a topee and was going blind,
Till I and the bird, the word and the tree, were one.

Richard Murphy

Seven Poems

For Anya On New Year's Day 1977

So far north, dim and short the gloomy day,
Did you imagine tree so grey could bear
Such a mauve bloom in black frost manacled
All winter sprawled on a grim iron bed?

Did you imagine you could make it flower,
Take in your hands the seawind's power to work
Gently against both time and soil to bring
A mass of memory springing from dead clay?

Yes, and where ridges choked with couch-grass lay
Still breeding spores of bitter famine blight,
You wrought my land's recovery, you made
Growth possible, put new words in my mouth.

Care

Kidded in April above Glencolumbkille
On a treeless hill backing north, she throve
Sucking milk off heather and rock, until

I came with children to buy her. We drove
South, passing Drumcliff. Restless in the car,
Bleating, she gulped at plastic teats we'd shove

Copiously in her mouth. Soon she'd devour
Whatever we'd give. Prettily she poked
Her gypsy head with hornbuds through barbed wire

To nip off pea-tops, her fawn pelt streaked
With Black Forest shadow and Alpine snow.
I stalled her wildness in a pen that locked.

She grew tame and fat, fed on herbs I knew
Her body needed. We ransacked Kylemore
To bring her oakleaf, ivy and bark to chew.

I gutted goatbooks, learning how to cure
Fluke, pulpy kidney, black garget, louping ill:
All my attention bled to cope with her.

No fenceless commonage to roam, no hill
Transfigured into cloud, no dragon wood
To forage with a puck-led flock: but the rattle

Of a bucket, shouts of children bringing food
Across a frozen yard. Out in a forest
She would have known a bad leaf from a good.

Here, captive to our taste, she'd learnt to trust
The petting hand with crushed oats, or a new
Mash of concentrates, or sweet bits of waste.

So when a child mistook a sprig of yew
And mixed it with her fodder, she descried
No danger: we had tamed her instinct too.

Whiskey, white of egg, linseed oil, we tried
Forcing down antidotes. Nothing would do.
The children came to tell me when she died.

Shelter

Girl with a sheaf of rye-straw in your arms
How much you carry from a loaded trailer
Parked at the door in a stray sunny shaft
At the tail end of summer, deep into the barn
To store for thatch, if ever we get the weather
Or the time, before winter sets in, how much
You help me, child, in the hour after school,
Hour of your release, face wet with tears
That well up out of a cruelty done to you,
Bruise-marks around your lips, a speechless harm,
How much you help me to make the dark inside
Glitter with sheaves bound firm to keep out storm.
Hear how they rustle as we lay them down:
Their broken heads are thrashed clean of grain.

Swallows

She wades through wet rushes,
Long autumn grass,
Over rusty barbed wire
And stone walls that collapse,

With a black rubber torch
That keeps flickering off,
After midnight, to reach
A shed with a tin roof.

She lifts away door-boards—
O sweet herbal hay!
Her beam dazzles birds
She can't identify.

Timorous wings in wormy rafters
Flap to get out.
Then she spots in a light-shaft
A red boot unlaced.

The flock's tremor increases
In her torch's coop.
Where is he? She sees
A white arm sticking up.

Mary Ure

Bare feet she dips across my boat's blue rail
In the ocean as we run under full white summer sail.
The cold spray kisses them. She's not immortal.

Sitting in her orchard she reads *Lady Lazarus*
Aloud rehearsing, when her smallest child lays
Red peonies in her lap with tender apologies.

She walks by Lough Mask in a blue silk gown
So thin the cloudy wind is biting to the bone
But she talks as lightly as if the sun shone.

Trouvaille

This root of bog-oak the sea dug up she found
Poking about, in old age, and put to stand
Between a snarling griffin and a half-nude man
Moulded of lead on my chimney-piece.
It looks like a heron rising from a pond,
Feet dipped in brown-trout water,
Head shooting arrow-sharp into blue sky.

"What does it remind you of?" she wanted to know.
I thought of trees in her father's demesne
Levelled by chainsaws;
Bunches of primroses I used to pick
Before breakfast, hunting along a limestone lane,
To put at her bedside before she woke;
And all my childhood's broken promises.

No, no! It precedes alphabets,
Planted woods, or gods.
Twisted and honed as a mind that never forgets
It lay dead in bog acids, undecayable:
Secretively hardening in a womb of moss, until
The peat burnt off, a freak tide raised
The feathered stick she took to lure me home.

Enigma

Her hair has a sweet smell of girlhood under his face
Darkening the moon on her pillow.

Tenderly her fingertips probe the furrows of his temple
And find the questionmark of an ear.

How can she play in the rubble of his pleasure ground
Paths overgrown with laurel and briar?

How can he pick the fruit she will bear in time to come
On her lips' not yet flowering bud?

Her future is an apple tree, his past a dark old yew
Growing together in this orchard now.

J.G. *Simms*

The Battle of Aughrim: History and Poetry

I
The Historian's View

Irish warfare has for the most part been an affair of skirmishes, raids and ambushes. There have been some notable sieges, but, by European standards, few battles between sizeable armies in regular formation. Aughrim was the last and bloodiest of them, the most dramatic, and, it can be argued, the most calamitous for the losing side. The Boyne, where King William put King James to flight, got more publicity and is better remembered today. But in a military sense Aughrim was the more significant. It was harder fought and claimed many more casualties. In a wider sense it decided, not only the war of 1689-91, but the shaping of Ireland for over two centuries. It was regularly commemorated throughout the eighteenth century and it gave birth to many legends and traditions. Jacobite and Williamite historians agree about its dramatic character and its importance, and have described its course in detail.

Aughrim was fought on Sunday 12 July 1691—by the old-style calendar; for the French it was 22 July. It came in the closing stages of 'the war of the two kings'. That war had gone on since James II came to Ireland in March 1689, hoping with French and Irish help to recover his English throne from his usurping son-in-law, William of Orange. For the French, the Irish operation was a peripheral manoeuvre in a European war between Louis XIV and an interdenominational alliance in which William and the Holy Roman Emperor were the leading figures. For Irish Catholics, King James and King Louis were chiefly important as providing support in what appeared to be a favourable opportunity to recover lost lands, status and religious freedom. The Elizabethan and Cromwellian conquests had placed political and economic power in the hands of a minority of Protestant settlers, and had subjected the religion of the Catholic majority to crippling restraints. In 1685 the accession of Catholic James offered the prospect that Catholics would become the dominant community. But no substantial change had been secured by the end of 1688, when the 'glorious revolution' in England again put the Catholics of Ireland in hazard. The resulting war would decide the issues—land, religion and political power, which for both Catholics and Protestants were nearer considerations than the fate of kings or the European balance of power. For both Catholics and Protestants the war had something of the character of a crusade.

It was a war of many ups and downs. The successful resistance of Protestant Derry and Enniskillen gave William's armies a secure bridgehead in Ulster. But William's general, Schomberg, failed to extend the bridgehead in the autumn of 1689 and allowed his men to die like flies in the marshes of Dundalk. William himself came to Ireland in 1690 and put James to flight at the Boyne on 1 July (old style). This gave him Dublin and most of Ireland up to the Shannon. But he had not destroyed the Jacobite army. Patrick Sarsfield emerged as a resolute leader, and William, after failing to take Limerick, returned to England, his work only half done. The Jacobites held the line of the Shannon for almost a year longer and Sarsfield, created Earl of Lucan, was the people's hero. But there was deep division of opinion. Richard Talbot, Duke of Tyrconnell, had thought it useless to resist after the Boyne and wise to make terms with William. A peace party hoped to bargain for land and religious toleration; a resistance party, headed by Sarsfield, countered their efforts. Rival delegations went to France. Louis decided to supply limited French aid and a French general.

In May 1691 the general arrived. He was Charles Chalmont, Marquis de St Ruth. His reputation had preceded him. In operations against the Protestants in Savoy his command had included the Irish regiments of MacCarthy, Dillon and O'Brien. St Ruth had thought highly of these Irish troops, and they had appreciated the enthusiasm with which he had campaigned against the heretics. He had earned the soubriquet of 'le missionaire botté' (the missionary in top boots).

St Ruth seems to have been of an arrogant and erratic temperament, and he was soon at loggerheads with both Tyrconnell and Sarsfield. His first test came in the latter part of June when Ginkel, William's Dutch general, attacked Athlone, which, after a stout resistance lasting several days, was taken by a sudden attack on 30 June. St Ruth, who was encamped with an army in the neighbourhood, was taken completely by surprise: "impossible, a town taken and I with an army to relieve it". The fall of Athlone breached the line of the Shannon and opened the way for Ginkel to attack Galway or Limerick, the two major towns still held by the Jacobites. Connacht was now at risk, and the prospect was grim for the Jacobites who had crowded into it from other parts of Ireland. Sarsfield was in favour of avoiding direct confrontation and of relying on cavalry raids behind the enemy lines. But St Ruth was determined to retrieve his reputation and to halt the Williamite advance by fighting a pitched battle. The shock of losing Athlone brought out the best in him, and he showed much skill in restoring morale in the Irish army and in choosing and preparing the site for the battle.

The site he chose was Kilcommodon hill, five miles south-west of Ballinasloe. It was an excellent choice. The hill commanded a wide prospect and was protected by a boggy stream from enemy advance. The only firm approaches were two narrow passages, to north and south. The northern passage, which carries the present road from Dublin to Galway, was a causeway skirting the bog and running near the old castle of Aughrim. The other was a ridge about a mile and a half to the south. Both approaches would be difficult for an enemy to force. The easy slope of Kilcommodon hill was intersected by hedges, and St Ruth ordered gaps to be cut in them to provide lines of communication from one part of the hill to another. What was left of the hedges was lined with musketeers ready to give a hot reception to such of the enemy as might succeed in struggling through the bog. There was an old rath—a Danesfort as it was called—near the top of the hill, which could serve St Ruth for headquarters, giving him a clear view across to the low hills that separated him from Ballinasloe. Drainage channels have made the bog less of an obstacle than it was then, but otherwise the landscape is little altered and it is not difficult to imagine the scene of battle.

The clearest of the contemporary accounts is that of the Rev. George Story, an Englishman who was present as chaplain to one of the Williamite regiments and whose two-part history of the campaign—*A True and Impartial History* (1691) and *A Continuation of the Impartial History* (1693)—represents a brave effort to deserve the adjectives in the titles. Story pays tribute to St Ruth's dexterity "in making choice of such a piece of Ground as Nature it self could not furnish him with a better".

St Ruth had been given plenty of time to prepare his position. Athlone had fallen on 30 June, but the cautious Ginkel did not reach Ballinasloe until 11 July. That day he himself went forward to rising ground from which he could see St Ruth's army on Kilcommodon hill. He had with him a map drawn by a member of the family of Trench—Huguenot La Tranches, who had settled at Garbally between Ballinasloe and Aughrim—and it is probable that

Story: *A True and Impartial History*, p. 135

this map provided the basis for the map in Story's book. Ginkel was impressed by the strength of the enemy position, but decided to challenge it on the following day. St Ruth was informed by his outposts of the enemy approach, and he too made ready for battle.

Story's map shows the Irish army drawn up in two lines about halfway up the hill, occupying a stretch of about two miles extending southwards from Aughrim castle to the Tristaun river below Kilcommodon church. St Ruth had two batteries of field guns, one on either side of his centre. The map appears to show a large body of troops in reserve to the west of Aughrim church. But the most recent, and most authoritative, historian of the battle has deduced that there was no such large reserve and has discounted the tradition that Sarsfield was placed in charge of it by a jealous St Ruth with instructions not to move without orders.[1] Perhaps the Williamites thought that there was such a reserve beyond their field of vision.

The map shows the Williamite army with its centre across the bog on the lower reaches of the hill and its right wing crossing the causeway and turning inwards opposite the castle. A large part of the Williamite army is shown on the left, on the pass leading to the Tristaun river. In the centre are two batteries on the slopes of the high ground of Urraghry overlooking the bog. Two other batteries are shown commanding the northern passage towards Aughrim castle.

From the Jacobite accounts we learn that St Ruth's centre consisted of infantry and that his cavalry were on the wings, protecting the passages at the northern and southern ends of the line. The more detailed of the two main Jacobite accounts is in a manuscript entitled "A Light to the Blind", attributed to a member of the Plunkett family and owned by the Earls of Fingall well into this century when it was acquired by the National Library of Ireland.[2] It represents the 'old English' point of view, that of the Catholic descendants of the Norman colonists. The other account is by Colonel Charles O'Kelly, a veteran soldier whose home was at Skryne (or Aughrane) castle, about sixteen miles north of Aughrim. He gave his account the peculiar title of "Macariae excidium, or the destruction of Cyprus". He disguised persons and places by giving them classical names: Cyprus standing

1. G.A. Hayes-McCoy, *Irish Battles* (London: Longmans Green & Co. Ltd., 1969), p. 250.
2. Edited by J. T. Gilbert as *A Jacobite Narrative of the War in Ireland 1688-1691* (Dublin, 1892; reprinted Shannon: Irish University Press, 1971).

for Ireland, Lysander for Sarsfield, and so on. Mercifully he supplied a key, and his editor, John Cornelius O'Callaghan, has used it for his marginal glosses.[3] O'Kelly represents the Gaelic Irish view, critical of the 'old English' as a set of self-interested quislings. It is unfortunate that he did not take a fuller opportunity of using his local knowledge to elaborate his account of the battle. These rival Jacobite histories show that there were strained relations between the Gaelic Irish and the 'old English' and that the latter were more ready to compromise with William in the hope of saving their property and being allowed the unobtrusive practice of their religion.

The Plunkett manuscript, which details the positions of individual regiments and commanders, says that the French lieutenant-general, de Tessé, was posted with the cavalry on the right and that Sarsfield was stationed with him. O'Kelly also says that de Tessé was in command on the right, but that Sarsfield commanded the cavalry on the left, or Aughrim, side. A Williamite account says that Sarsfield was placed in the rear with instructions not to move without orders. De Tessé's own despatch shows that he assumed command after St Ruth's death and makes no reference at all to Sarsfield.

Every effort seems to have been made to create a crusading spirit in the Irish army. As it was Sunday, masses were said on the hillside and priests were present in great numbers to pray and preach. A Catholic bishop later wrote to a friend in Rome that eighty priests were killed carrying crucifixes and urging the troops to fight for their faith. The Plunkett manuscript refers to an address given by St Ruth to his army on the previous day, presumably through an interpreter. Story prints *in extenso* what was claimed to be a copy of the address, found in the pocket of the dead general's dead secretary, though Story himself had doubts of its authenticity.

Story gives Ginkel's order of battle: two lines with cavalry on the wings. His army was multinational, reflecting the European character of the conflict. There was a large contingent hired from the king of Denmark, and several Huguenot and Dutch regiments. The rest were English, or regiments formed from Ulster Protestants, veterans of Derry and Enniskillen. Both armies were about 20,000 strong. Ginkel had the advantage in artillery, but the Irish army had much the better position.

The early part of the day was taken up with inconclusive skirmishing. The real fight did not begin until 5 pm when Ginkel

3. Edited by J.C. O'Callaghan (Dublin:–, 1850).

sent Danish and Huguenot foot across the southern part of the bog to attack the right of the Irish infantry. This was hard going, first through marshes, then up to the hedges and ditches on the lower slopes of the hill. The Irish resisted strongly. In Story's words they "behaved themselves like Men of another Nation, defending their Ditches stoutly". The site of the fight is still known as the 'bloody hollow'. To support his hard-pressed right St Ruth switched units from his left (or Aughrim) side. Ginkel countered by sending four English regiments through the northern part of the bog nearest to the Aughrim causeway. Here was the fiercest fighting of the day. The men had to struggle through streams and bog, up to their waists in mud and water. As they emerged on to dry ground, they were assaulted by Irish horse and foot and driven back as far as the battery of guns that Ginkel had placed on his own side of the bog. The Irish, lighter of foot, pursued them with clubbed muskets. Colonel Gordon O'Neill's men made a temporary capture of some guns. St Ruth was delighted and, according to the Plunkett manuscript, cried out: *"le jour est à nous, mes enfants"*. Ginkel's desperate remedy was to order an advance across the narrow causeway towards Aughrim castle. Ruvigny, the Huguenot cavalry commander who later became Earl of Galway, led the way across the perilous ridge to what the Plunkett account calls "an old broken causeway, only large enough for two horses to pass it at a time". The cavalry on the Irish left and the defenders of the castle should have made the causeway impassable, but, in Story's words, Ruvigny's horse "did extraordinary service, bearing down all before them". They cleared the way for infantry to follow and turn inwards across the hill, taking the Irish in the flank.

St Ruth saw what was happening, ordered reinforcements to move to the Aughrim side, and himself rode in that direction. At that moment a cannon ball took off his head. De Tessé, who took over command, later reported that the news of this disaster created such consternation among the infantry in the centre that they had no thought but flight. De Tessé tried to rally them, without success. He was wounded, but not seriously, and seems to have left the field without handing over to Sarsfield or anyone else. It was left to Sarsfield and Lord Galmoy to cover the retreat as best they could, but the pursuing Williamites were able to inflict horrible slaughter on the fleeing Irish.

It was a calamitous reversal of fortune. Both Jacobite accounts lay great stress on the death of St Ruth. O'Kelly records it as the general opinion that if St Ruth had lived an hour longer, the Irish would have won the day. The Plunkett account lamented that the cannon ball that struck St Ruth "laid the nation prostrate at his feet". The same account blamed the Irish cavalry for giving up the struggle. The writer's contempt was expressed in a withering phrase: "and so let them keep their *priding cavalry* to stop bottles with". The cavalry had been entrusted with the defence of the Aughrim causeway and should have stood their ground. Instead, Brigadier Luttrell withdrew "after a small resistance". The stretch of road leading from Aughrim towards Galway became known as Luttrell's Pass, and Luttrell, who was later found to be in communication with Ginkel and received a pension from William for his services, was branded as the arch-traitor. He and other cavalry commanders had estates to lose or keep, and they appear to have thought it time to make terms with the enemy.

Aughrim was a complete disaster. The flower of the Irish army was destroyed there and many famous families lost their sons. Poets lamented the dead and gave the place the name *Eachroim an áir*—Aughrim of the slaughter. Galway surrendered a few days later and Limerick, the last stronghold, surrendered in less than three months. Ginkel's victorious campaign was followed by confiscation of land, penal laws, and two centuries of Protestant ascendancy.

Would things have been different but for that fatal cannon ball? St Ruth might well have turned the scales against that daring advance of Ginkel's men across the causeway and cut communications between them and their main army. But even if the Irish army had got the better of Ginkel that day, it is hard to believe that the eventual outcome of the war would have been very different. The line of the Shannon had been breached and the Irish were trapped in a Connacht that had become highly vulnerable; they were inferior to their opponents in equipment and supplies; the issues at stake meant much more to William and his supporters than they did to the French, on whom the Irish had to rely for the sinews of war. At best, the war might have been prolonged into the following year, or terms might have been offered by Ginkel that would have left the Williamites in control but under conditions less harsh for Jacobites. The course of history did not turn on one man's life.

II
The Poet's View

When we turn to Richard Murphy's poem on Aughrim, we are in
a different world. The historian is preoccupied with problems of
documentary evidence, chronology and rational analysis, and with
the effort to present the appearance of objective detachment. In
the poet's world, present and past are one, identification is
preferred to detachment, instinct is more than intellect.

For both historian and poet, the battle is more than the firing
of guns and the slaughter of men; for both it is a conflict of ideas
and interests, religious fervour and pride of race, the possession of
houses and lands, continuity with the past and anxiety for the
future. But the treatment is different. The prosaic narrative of the
historian sets out the issues in as orderly a way as possible in an
attempt to impose form on the formless. The poet is not bound by
documents or rules of space and time; he is freer to make use of
traditions, other men's songs or his own fancy. But he has also
familiarised himself with the documents that the historian has
used, such as contemporary narratives or correspondence, and he
has read the writings of successive historians. His poem has echoes
of phrases quoted or used in past narratives. Familiarity with the
history adds to the pleasure of those who read the poem and
savour the allusions.

The poem is in four sections: Now, Before, During and After.
'Now' is a series of impressions formed by the poet during the
gestation of his poem. He begins with the summer landscape,
changed, but not utterly, from that of the summer of 1691. The
bog is drained, tractors and earth-movers are far away from the
seventeenth century. But the eskar ridge is there, the ditches and
hedges that once were stubbornly defended, and the stream
through Luttrell's Pass, "passed by cavalry traitors". The Celtic
cross that "commemorates no battle/But someone killed in a car,
Minister of Agriculture" has by its incongruity impressed the poet
more than the taller cross belatedly put up in 1961 (after lying
for half a century in the street of Ballinasloe) in memory of St
Ruth and those who fell at Aughrim.

As always, Richard Murphy's writing is marked by a strong
sense of detail. Close observation and a highly visual imagination
give a sharp focus to the picture. He knows the history, has seen
the museum of bullets and muskets lovingly arranged by Master
Joyce, and has ridden to the bush that marks the spot where St
Ruth was killed. The view from Kilcommodon hill is in essence

that of Story's map. The modern Aughrim is out of sight, and the opposing slopes, with the intervening streams and marsh not wholly drained, are free of buildings. The eye of a poet, or of a historian, can people the tract with colourful armies, smoking guns, and the killed and wounded in 'bloody hollow'. The 'Now' of Aughrim is the continuing alienation of the vanquished and the victors, symbolised by the plaques in "the rival churches". The poet, with his Gaelic patronymic and his Cromwellian ancestor, can identify with both victor and vanquished. It was for ownership of the land that the leaders on either side fought that day, and the opening words of the poem at once make the point:

Who owns the land where musket-balls are buried
In blackthorn roots on the eskar, the drained bogs
Where sheep browse, and credal war miscarried?

The result of the battle was to decide that the land would be owned by the descendants of the victors until this century, when they were paid to surrender it so that it could be divided among the descendants of the vanquished. One of the consequences of Aughrim was the absentee landlord of whom the old woman in the poem spoke:

Aughrim's great disaster
Made him two hundred years my penal master.

For the landless men who fought on either side in 1691, the "credal war" counted for more than the contest for landed property. The poem reminds us that the effects of Aughrim are discernible in the Northern conflict:

In bowler hats and Sunday suits,
Orange sashes, polished boots,
Atavistic trainbands come
To blow the fife and beat the drum.

Apprentices uplift their banner
True blue-dyed with 'No Surrender!'
Claiming Aughrim as if they'd won
Last year, not 1691.

But though Aughrim has a place on the Orange banners of today, it gets less than its due from a festival in which the descendants of the Enniskilleners and Derrymen celebrate King Billy and their other victory, the Boyne.

How long was the poem in gestation? In 1962, six years before it saw the light, the poet met seekers after military history, fresh from studying Ginkel's campaign, when one of the "new elite" of the Irish army proudly showed a bullet "Lodged in a skull" at Aughrim. The poem was still in the making when "Casement's skeleton" came flying home in the early part of 1965. "This rebel quixote" forms part of the 'Now' of Aughrim, honoured with a funeral for his effort in 1916 to reverse the verdict of 1691.

'Before' is the poet's impression of Aughrim before the battle: of the two armies divided not only by red bogs but by "godly bigotry and pride of race". The section opens with a reference to a poem written two hundred and fifty years ago "in a language that has died". The language of which Richard Murphy was thinking was Irish, but no poem in Irish tells the full story of the battle, though there are elegies for some of its high-born victims. Another language that has died—if either can be called dead—is used in the Latin hexameters of a Jacobite poem on the war, which gives a Homeric sense of combat between opposing heroes to the fierce fighting at Aughrim.[4]

Next we get, in an interval of prose, the whole speech that George Story hesitantly attributed to St Ruth. But, if we discount the boastful self-praise with which it begins, the speech does illuminate the issues: "You are not Mercinary Souldiers, you do not fight for your Pay, but for your Lives, your Wives, your Children, your Liberties, your Countrey, your Estates; and to restore the most Pious of Kings to his Throne: But above all for the propagation of the Holy Faith, and the subversion of Heresie." After that we are reminded how the war hits ordinary men and women, the pregnant lover of Sarsfield's trooper, the couple at the well hanged by Williamite soldiers who suspect them of poisoning the water.

Then comes the incident of which the tradition was told last century to John Cornelius O'Callaghan: of the farmer Kelly and his shepherd Mullen, who got no payment from St Ruth for commandeered sheep, and crossed the bog to Ginkel's army, vowing vengeance on the Frenchman. On the Protestant side there is the Cromwellian landlord, determined to preserve the yews that he planted forty years ago. To him the issue of the battle is the

4. The section on Aughrim is published as an appendix to J.T. Gilbert's edition of *A Jacobite Narrative of the War in Ireland 1688-1691*.

ownership of the land made fertile by his care. With the land went gracious living: silver candlesticks, a polished table, and a daughter playing Purcell on the harpsichord. The landlord was an ancestor of the poet. He was Robert Miller of Ballycushin, County Mayo, and in the family tradition his contribution to Ginkel's victory was to entertain Balldearg—"red-mouthed" (or should it have been "red-mark"?)—O'Donnell until the traitor slept, while his thousand clansmen waited far from the battlefield. 'Before' ends with the rapparees, the ubiquitous partisans who were a continuous menace to the Williamites, hiding in streams by day like otters—the phrase is Story's—, burning houses and raiding castles by night:

The water is still. A rock or the nose of an otter
Jars the surface. Whistle of rushes or bird?
It steers to the bank, it lands as a pikeman armed.

'During' makes no attempt to describe the movement of troops or the tide of battle. It is a succession of equestrian portraits: St Ruth, Sarsfield, and the traitor Luttrell.

St Ruth trots on a silver mare
Along the summit of the ridge,
Backed by a red cavalcade
Of the King's Life Guards.
He wears a blue silk tunic,
A white lace cravat,
Grey feathers in his hat.

It is the poet's imagination that gives St Ruth his silver mare, his fine clothes, his jowls that "bleach and blush/Like a turkey-cock's dewlap", and a "long forked nose/Acclimatised to the sulphurous/Agony of Huguenots." We have no portrait of St Ruth, but St Simon's spiteful memoirs record that he was monstrously ugly and incurably addicted to wife-beating. The verses that tell of his death follow the tradition of the farmer Kelly and the shepherd Mullen pointing out St Ruth to Ginkel's gunner:

Chance, skill and treachery all hit the mark
Just when the sun's rod tipped the altar hill:
The soldiers panicked, thinking God had struck.

But a modern historian, versed in the weakness of seventeenth-century artillery, has discounted all but chance. An elaboration of the story—not alluded to in the poem—tells that the gun could not be raised to the required elevation until Trench took the heel off his boot and inserted it under the muzzle. Trench was rewarded for his war service with the deanery of Raphoe, and an Orange toast of the eighteenth century was "to the heel of the Dean of Raphoe's boot".

St Ruth fills the picture and the contending armies are in the shadows. But in a sense this is justifiable distortion: St Ruth dominated the battle in the minds both of the Irish and of their opponents. Charles O'Kelly's account of the battle is little more than a lament for St Ruth, the beloved general, the irreparable loss. The Williamite Story pays grudging tribute to St Ruth: "tho the man had an ill Character in being one of the greatest Persecutors of the Protestants in France, yet, we must allow him to be very brave in his Person, and indeed considerable in his Conduct, since he brought the Irish to fight a better Battle, than ever their Nation could boast of before." A verse drama, popular among Protestants in the eighteenth century, had the title "The battle of Aughrim, or the fall of Monsieur St Ruth".[5]

Then we have Sarsfield, riding a chestnut horse, "His mountainous green shoulders/Tufted with gold braid". A historian, if indeed he mentioned the shoulders, would have made them red. Sarsfield was in a British army and held his commission from King James. But in another sense the shoulders were green; they belonged to an Irish hero, the darling of an army that took little account of Seamus a' Chaca, James the Shit. The poem accepts the version that relegated Sarsfield to the reserve, ignorant of the battle plan, forbidden to move without orders. There is some evidence to support this version, which is accepted by the Jacobite poem in Latin hexameters: "when the commander was killed, the password and order of battle had been committed to none of the leaders, not to Lucan himself." In the final stages of the battle, all that Sarsfield can do is to try to cover a retreat that had become a rout:

> He sees men run on the skyline
> Throwing away muskets and pikes,
> Then horsemen with sabres drawn
> Cutting them down.

5.   By Robert Ashton. It went through twenty-two editions between 1740 and 1764.

He hears cries, groans and shrieks.
Nothing he will do, or has done
Can stop this happening.

There is irony in the fact that Ireland's hero did no more than
cover the retreat at both the Boyne and Aughrim.
Lastly we have:

Luttrell on a black charger
At the rear of his regiment
Stands idle in a beanfield
Protected by a tower.
He wears a dandy yellow coat,
A white-feathered hat
And a gilded sabre.

When he hears the word spread
Along the line, 'St Ruth is dead',
He retreats at a trot:
Leading his priding cavalry
To betray the humble foot:
Ten miles to a dinner, laid
In a mansion, then to bed.

Besides these three leading actors, we have the defenders of the
castle who were sent "Irish bullets too large for French firelocks"
and reduced to firing tunic buttons, though the buttons do not get
into the record till fifty years later. The final picture is a grim
reconstruction of a brutal encounter between English troopers and
a wounded Irish boy.

'After' begins with the story of the faithful wolfhound guarding
his master's body. This comes straight from Story's history, except
that in his version the dog was a greyhound. Story also supplies
the next item, musing about the fate of St Ruth's corpse and
about the Irish whose genius was to rebel and whose vice was
laziness: 'Give one a cow and a potato garden/He will aspire to no
greater wealth/But loiter on the highway to hear news.'' The
sentiments and most of the words are Story's but there has been
some cutting and trimming to convert the *Impartial History* into
something that looks like blank verse.

There follows an imaginative description of Henry Luttrell,
master of Luttrellstown on the outskirts of Dublin, who was
indeed killed in 1717 in his sedan chair in a Dublin street—belated

vengeance for the treachery of 1691. Sarsfield appears again with a sketch of his earlier career, his role at Aughrim, and his departure with the "wild geese" to die on a foreign field, though historians doubt whether his last words were "Would to God this wound had been for Ireland." The end is the return of the wild geese in the form of tourists landing at Shannon for a quick visit to Aughrim and "the dun/Where St Ruth spun the thread of his fatal plan".

* * *

History and poetry need one another. The poet could not have written as he did without the work of historians old and new. But history gains from the imagination of the poet: making the dry bones live, putting twopence coloured in place of penny plain, distilling the essence from a confusion of documents and detailed narratives. I have been glad to use Richard Murphy's poem in the teaching of history, and those whom I have taught have gained insights from it that could not so readily be communicated in prose. His poem gives individuality to the figureheads of Aughrim and to the nameless groups they led; it gives speech to the thoughts and feelings that moved men and women ten generations ago. It is salutary for students of history to realise that there is more than one way of interpreting the past.

Tradition and imagination have a legitimate part to play in supplementing the fragmentary records and one-sided narratives consulted by historians who write about the seventeenth century.

Can it be said that Richard Murphy has drawn a distorted picture of Aughrim? I do not think so. His presentation is subjective, but the subjectivity is balanced. His sources are taken from the literature and folklore of both sides, with no obvious leaning to one or the other. He has taken note of treachery, cruelty and the fate of harmless countryfolk in grim descriptions that do not require moral judgements on his part. He does not administer praise or blame. This historian finds himself in sympathy with the poet's sense that a whole people was caught up in a dispute that on one level represented the rivalries of kings and churches, on another a struggle between opposing groups for the ownership of land. The chief consequence for Ireland of the war in which Aughrim was the last and deciding battle was the establishment of a Protestant ascendancy, based on the possession of lands that had been taken from the Catholic nobility and gentry who had supported the losing side. The change of masters affected generations of those who worked the land. The Protestant victory created a divided society which has not yet become completely integrated. The poet himself is the heir of divided traditions, and is looking for his own identity.

Michael Herity

The High Island Hermitage

A shoulder of rock
Sticks high up out of the sea,
A fisherman's mark
For lobster and blue-shark.

High Island, the Ard Oilean of Colgan, Ware and O'Flaherty, lies beyond Friar's Island and two miles west of Aughrus Point in Connemara, the most westerly land in County Galway. North of it are the larger islands of Inishark and Inishbofin, south is Cruagh Island and, sheltered in an angle south of the Aughrusbeg peninsula, Omey Island, which is joined to the mainland except at high tide. The highest point of this block of mica schist which is High Island is 208 feet above the sea and it slopes from about this height at the north end to about eighty feet at the south. Its coast is much indented and consists for the most part of overhanging cliffs which make landing impossible except in two relatively sheltered coves at the north-east end of the island. Eighty acres of undulating grassland have supported large numbers of sheep within living memory; three tiny lakes and two wells provided water for them.

It has long been uninhabited. The last people to live permanently on the island were the miners who for some years beginning in 1828 dug copper for the local landlord, Colonel Martin of Ballynahinch, out of the deep shaft a short way above the landing place.[1] They lived in two houses nearby, which were marked as 'Ruins' on the Ordnance Survey Fair Plan in 1839.[2] The much-ruined hermitage at the further end of the island was founded by St Fechin (600-664), who had earlier founded the little monastery on Omey and whose name, Latinised *Festus*, is still given at baptism to many of the boys in the locality.

The monastery is sited in a hollow at the south-west and most remote end of the island, beside the largest of the lakes. Here is

1. G.H. Kinahan, J. Nolan, H. Leonard and B.J. Cruise, *Explanatory Memoir of the Geological Survey of Ireland illustrating the Geological Structure of the District around Clifden, Connemara* (Dublin: Alexander Thom; Hodges, Foster and Co., 1878), p. 162.
2. I am indebted to the Director of the Ordnance Survey for permission to consult the manuscript Fair Plan of the Six-Inch Map at the Ordnance Survey Office and to Mr Seán Ó Nualláin, Archaeology Officer, for his help in interpreting it.

Fig. 1. High Island hermitage, *clochán* E, from the north-east.

almost as far as one can reach from the landing place. West lies only the Atlantic; the only part of the mainland to be seen lies low on the horizon away to the south-east at Slyne Head. The island of Inishark, on the north side, can be seen only by climbing a little way out of the hollow, and it is then framed between the cliff-like edges of a great indent the sea has made there, only fifty metres from the monastery itself; and the most awesome of three at this end of the island. To see further north and south, one must climb well to the north above the monastic enclosure, when the island appears as one of a great chain of islands stretching south from Achill: Clare Island, Caher Island, Inishturk, Inishark and Inishbofin, many of which had at one time remote monasteries similar to that of High Island. Despite this impression of being part of a chain of islands, the dominant feeling is one of isolation and remoteness, of subjection to the power of the sea.

The High Island foundation, thus remote from the world, is brought close to nature. The sea in its benign moods laps the rocks which reach down towards it at this end of the island and from which one could fish and swim with ease. In its savage moods, driven by gales from the west or north, its sound on the cliffs and inlets on all sides must have been terrifying for the hermits, and the whole enclosure must have been washed with sea-spray. Whereas in good weather there is shelter from most breezes below the declivity under which the monastery sits, one could hardly hope for more than a little relief in a storm. In springtime, the storm petrel nests among the ruined stones of the monastery, and the pink thrift and the white sea-campion flourish. It is easy to recreate there the ambience in which the nature poetry of the Early Christian period was written.

The descriptions of this tiny monastery of St Fechin date from the nineteenth century. They were written by George Petrie in 1820,[3] John O'Donovan in June 1839,[4] G. H. Kinahan [5] and R. A. S. Macalister.[6] None of these appears to have spent more than a few hours on the island but all, with the probable exception of Macalister, were able to see the ruins in a much better state of preservation than they are now, and their observations of certain details are therefore valuable. No proper plan has been made; the Ordnance Survey, unhappily, did not do one, and Kinahan's sketch-plan is misleading since he confuses the inner and the outer enclosures. I therefore welcome the opportunity to put on record a tentative plan and reconstruction of this ruined but striking hermitage, based on fieldwork done in the summer of 1976, with a short consideration of its context.

Despite the destruction of the nineteenth century, which local tradition suggests was wrought by the miners in search of building stone, the High Island monastery is one of the few relatively well-preserved island monasteries that exist today. Unlike many other monasteries, it seems to be free of later burials. It appears also to have retained its primitive form without significant change throughout the four centuries during which it was certainly in use. It is thus an important document in the reconstruction of the earliest phases of Christian building in Ireland.

> Dark mounds of mica schist,
> A lake, mill and chapel,
> Roofless, one gable smashed,
> Lie ringed with rubble.

3. George Petrie, *The Ecclesiastical Architecture of Ireland* (Dublin: Hodges and Smith, 1845), pp. 128-29, 419-22, 441.
4. *Ordnance Survey Letters, County Galway*, pp. 75-87.
5. G.H. Kinahan, "The Ruins on Ardillaun, Co Galway", *Proceedings of the Royal Irish Academy*, 10 (1866-69), 551-55.
6. R.A.S. Macalister, "The Antiquities of Ardillaun, County Galway", *Journal of the Royal Irish Society of Antiquaries of Ireland*, 26 (1896), 197-210.

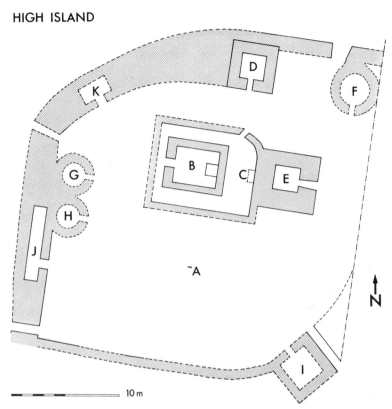

Fig.2. Reconstructed plan of the hermitage at High Island; additions based on the nineteenth-century descriptions shown with broken lines.

The hermitage is a walled enclosure, roughly quadrangular in shape, sited in a hollow on the edge of the largest of the three lakes and built of the dark slaty schist of the island. Its south wall was built straight along the edge of the lake, and originally was probably no more than 80 cm thick. The wall on the east side apparently faced an edge scarped out from a natural terrace rising steeply above it and was again virtually straight. On the west and north sides there is a substantial curved wall about 3 m thick, wide enough to incorporate two wall-chambers in its fabric. There are four entrances, in the north-east, north-west, south-west and south-east corners, and the area enclosed is quite small, its longest and shortest axes measuring 35 and 28 metres. (Fig. 2).

The southern half of the enclosure, nearest the lake, is clear of buildings. Within this open space, in a central position stands a

Fig. 3. High Island hermitage, cross-slab in the open space within the enclosure.

cross-slab [A] of schist with its design in the south side, facing the lake (Fig. 3). The right-hand, eastern edge has been broken off. The date of the design need not be much later than the year 700; it might even belong to the time of the foundation of Fechin in the middle of the seventh century. Nearby is a sphere of granite 46 cm across. This part of the enclosure, then, was an open, public place with the cross-slab as its focus.

In the northern half of the enclosure stood the principal building, the oratory [B], with the other buildings of the monastery grouped around it. This tiny oratory was built in the conventional orientation, its simple battered doorway facing north of west and a tiny window above an altar in the opposite wall facing south of east. The internal measurements are 4 m long by 3.2 m broad, the building therefore being almost square in shape. The lintel now over the doorway is a re-used cross-slab and above this the gable is built in a much cruder masonry than the lower courses: it is therefore a reconstruction. There is now no trace of the roofing or its supports but it probably was of conventional timber-framed construction.

A rare and noteworthy feature of the oratory is the rectangular walled enclosure which surrounds it. Though much ruined and masked by falling stones, it appears to follow the rectangular outline of the church, ranging between 1.20 and 2.70m in distance from it. The area inside formed a sheltered walkway around the oratory. It was in the wider space at the eastern end of this walkway that Petrie saw in 1820 "an ancient stone sepulchre like a pagan kistvaen, composed of large mica slates with a cover of limestone".[7] The end-stones were "rudely sculptured with ornamental crosses and a human figure" and the covering-slab was also carved [C]. From its prominent position and elaborate ornamentation, I take this to be probably the tomb of the founder or first abbot. The only entrance discernible in the surrounding wall is in the north-east corner and it has a rude corbelled arch over it. Petrie records "a covered passage about 15ft long by 3ft wide"; traces of this can be discerned today, leading past the doorway of the stone cell opposite to the north-east entrance. The enclosure and its approach passage mark the structures within and near it as having a special significance.

The stone wall or *clochán* in the north wall [D] is unique in that its entrance faces the entrance to this enclosure. It has a rectilinear base, 2.2m square on the inside, and its roof is a stone beehive superimposed on this. Its position suggests that it housed the most important personage of the monastery, the abbot or principal guest. The second of the two remaining *clocháns* [E] is built onto the outside of the enclosing wall of the oratory on the east side and is roughly the same size. Its doorway faces east and away from the oratory. Petrie[8], Kinahan[9] and O'Donovan[10] each did drawings of this cell, which has massive walls and a large splayed entrance. Perhaps it was a communal building, a scriptorium or refectory.

There is evidence from the older accounts of three further buildings within the enclosure. O'Donovan in a pencilled description in the Ordnance Survey Namebook,[11] and Kinahan[12] both described a ruined *clochán* apparently in the angle beside the

7. Petrie, *Ecclesiastical Architecture*, p. 420.
8. ibid., p. 128.
9. Kinahan, *Ruins on Ardillaun*, Pl. XLVIII.
10. *Ordnance Survey Letters, Co Galway*, p. 81.
11. I am indebted to the Director of the Ordnance Survey for permission to consult the Namebook at the Ordnance Survey Office, Dublin.
12. Kinahan, *Ruins on Ardillaun*, 553.

north-east entrance; O'Donovan makes it 12 feet long by 9 feet broad, Kinahan about 9 feet square. It may have been a gatehouse [F]. Petrie refers to "a number of smaller cells" on the west side of the chapel. Two are tentatively indicated in this area at [G] and [H] in the sketch plan (Fig. 2). The remains of another building guard the south-east entrance [I] but this is different in that it is rectangular with relatively thin walls and is placed outside the enclosure.

A very fine corbelled wall-chamber [J], 6.6 by 1.2m, referred to by Kinahan as The Prison,[13] runs under the enclosing wall in the south-west quadrant. Its doorway is in the south-east corner. Kinahan describes a similar smaller chamber, "nine feet long by four and a half feet wide" in the wall north of the north-west entrance [K], but no trace of this is visible today since this part of the wall is almost completely ruined.

The High Island hermitage is therefore a simple enclosure with an oratory and a handful of stone huts, the two huts remaining being, with the oratory, the principal buildings of the establishment. The focal points of the enclosure were the oratory, the tomb on the east side of it and the stone cross-slab to the south. The wall surrounding the oratory and tomb is unique and intriguing, the more so since it was apparently approached by a covered passageway. The whole establishment can hardly have housed more than ten devotees.

North of the hermitage, between it and the cliff, is a small triangular garden about 40m long by 25m broad at the base. Its east side is bounded by a wall continuing from the east wall of the monastery; above this a clearly marked lynchet has formed from the accumulation of earth washed from the slope above it. The wall on the west side is now only faintly marked. On the edge of the cliff, at the apex of this triangle, are the remains of a rectangular building [L] now marked only by the low upright stones of the wall foundations. Beside this was the entrance through the wall to the enclosure.[14]

About 60m east, outside the monastery and this enclosing wall, overlooking it and sheltered by high ground on the east and south, is a circular stone enclosure about 8m across. Its entrance is apparently in the north-west, facing the hermitage, and it commands a much better view of sea and land than the hermitage below. Perhaps this was a guest-house [M].

The larger lake beside the hermitage empties itself into the sea

13. ibid., 554.
14. ibid., 552.

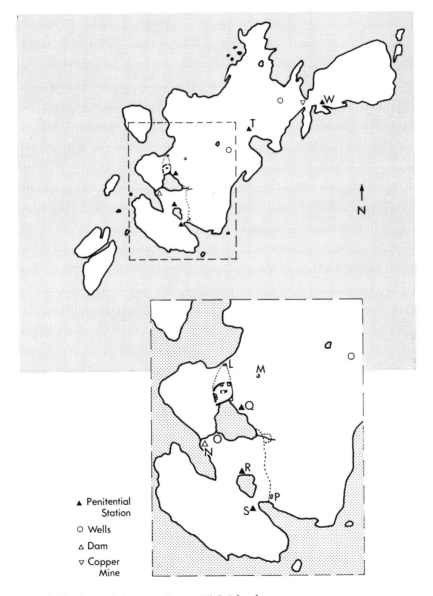

Fig. 4. Early Christian remains on High Island.

through a small stream which runs out of it on the western side. At its end, above the sea, stands a rectilinear drystone structure, apparently part of a dam for controlling the water level at the outflow [N]. Kinahan refers to this as a mill-dam, stating that a mill which stood here in ancient times had gone by his day.[15] A small pond about 3m by 2m was formed by building an L-shaped wall against the edge of the lake immediately south of the outflow; was this a flax-pond? [O].

A second, smaller lake stands a little to the south of this larger one. Even in the extremely dry summer of 1976 neither of these lakes dried up, although a third one higher up at the west end of the island did. Both were cut off from the rest of the island by a stone wall running roughly south from the south-east corner of the larger lake and ending close to the sea in the foundations of a rectangular building [P] not unlike that at the northern entrance to the monastery. This is a rectangular heap of stones [Q] with, standing at one end of it, an anthropomorphic cross-slab. Between the two lakes is a tiny enclosure [R], about 3m by 2m overall, not mentioned in the older descriptions. The third [S] stands on the edge of the sea, a little distance south of the smaller lake, and now has a holed stone set up beside it.

Fig. 5. Brian Boru's Well, High Island, cleaned out by Richard Murphy in the summer of 1969.

15.   ibid., 555.

Fig. 6. Cross-slab W above the landing-place, High Island.

There are two further penitential stations on the island. The first [T] is in the centre, near Brian Boru's Well, and is marked by a slab which has a cross with expanded arms incised on both faces. The second [W] is above the landing place and is marked by a slab engraved with a small Latin cross. Opposite the arms of the cross, the edges of the slab have two slight expansions and on the narrow edge beside the left-hand arm is a small Maltese cross, deeply incised.

Two other ancient walls remain to be noted; these are short stretches of stone wall, one running across the narrow neck of land above the landing place, and a second near the lake at the west end of the island. They indicate that the ancient inhabitants of the island practised some form of animal management.

* * *

Men digging down at St Fechin's church,
Buried in sand for centuries
Up to its pink stone gable top, a perch
For choughs and seapies.

On the north side of Omey Island, in a little hollow sheltered on the west and north by rocks and now covered in blown sand, is *Teampall Fechín*, the church of Fechin, who is said to have converted the inhabitants of Omey from paganism and set up this foundation before going on to High Island. Nearby is a burial ground. It was here that Colgan, the sixteenth-century hagiographer, found one ·of the three manuscript lives of Fechin on which he based his own.[16]

The east gable and part of the north wall are now exposed. Both are built almost entirely of the local pink granite, originally squared and mortared with a good shell mortar. In the centre of the gable is the standard single window, which has an embrasure about a metre wide on the inner side. This is a much larger building than the simple oratory on High Island, being about 4.50m in width, and in its present form is probably much later in date. Its position opposite High Island, on what is virtually the mainland, suggests that this was the landing-point for the hermits of the island. Similar mainland churches are situated opposite island hermitages on the west coast, at Streedagh opposite Inishmurray in County Sligo, and at Temple Cashel[17] above St Finan's Bay and opposite the monastery on the larger Skellig in County Kerry. These foundations were probably built to provide a monastic ambience for the hermits if they were cut off by bad weather from their own monastery on the island.

* * *

Simple monasteries of the kind found on High Island are sited all along the west coast of Ireland, particularly on the islands. Their history is normally brief, their lore almost as slight. Frequently the only trace of art is found on the cross-slab, which is always a prominent monument, and their buildings show a minimum of architectural elaboration. Besides the tiny rectangular oratory, beehive cells of stone (*clocháns*) are found,

16.   James F. Kenney, *The Sources for the Early History of Ireland; Ecclesiastical: An Introduction and Guide.* (reprinted New York: Octagon Books, 1966), pp. 459-60.
17.   Francoise Henry, "Early Monasteries, Beehive Huts and Drystone Houses in the Neighbourhood of Cahirciveen and Waterville, Co Kerry", *Proceedings of the Royal Irish Academy*, 58C (1957), 106.

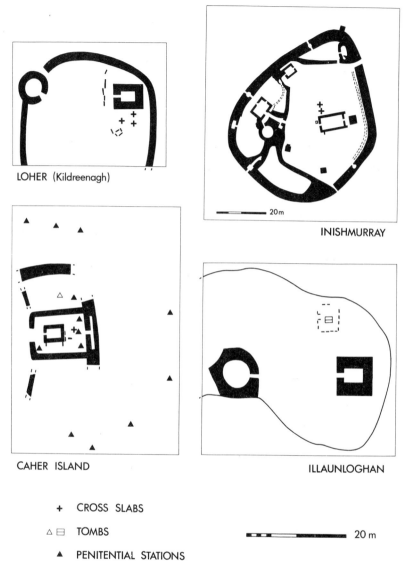

LOHER (Kildreenagh)

INISHMURRAY

20 m

CAHER ISLAND

ILLAUNLOGHAN

+   CROSS SLABS

△ 🖻   TOMBS   20 m

▲   PENITENTIAL STATIONS

Fig. 7. Simplified plans of parts of Early Christian monasteries at Kildreenagh, Loher townland, near Waterville, Co Kerry, Inishmurray, Co Sligo, Caher Island, Co Mayo and Illaunloghan, near Portmagee, Co Kerry. All after Henry, except Inishmurray, which is drawn from Wakeman's plan and is reproduced at half the scale of the others.

sometimes, as at High Island, with a rectilinear base and a circular beehive roof. Their simplicity suggests that their builders were drawn by the ideals of the primitive and the ascetic and that their communities were extremely conservative. They contrast strongly with the developed monastic towns of the midlands and east of the country, like Monasterboice, Fore and Kells, with their more spacious buildings and elaborate High Crosses, which grew and evolved in the centuries up to 900 and again in the eleventh and twelfth centuries, and even later, in response to changing fashion.

The cross-slab now standing in the open space south of the oratory in the High Island hermitage is the only feature of the complex capable of being closely dated [A]. Its design is the same as that of the medallions of the gilt-bronze belt shrine, also from an ecclesiastical milieu, found at Moylough, County Sligo.[18] This shrine is dated to the eighth century, so the slab need not be more than half a century later in date than the foundation of the hermitage by Fechin, say in 650. A similarly early cross-slab stands in Gannew townland at the thirteenth station of St Colmcille's *turas* or penitential round at Glencolumbkille in County Donegal.[19] This slab can be dated by its close similarity in design to that of a glass stud made to take a metal inset, and found in its clay mould in the lake-dwelling of Lagore in County Meath,[20] which in turn resembles the decorative studs of the eighth-century Ardagh Chalice.[21]

The Donegal slab indicates that the custom of the *turas* or pilgrimage-round of penitential stations may be as old as Christianity itself in Ireland, and the penitential stations in the vicinity of the High Island hermitage may be of similar antiquity. This may also be true of some of the stations indicated inside and around the Caher Island hermitage.[22] In this custom of the *turas* may lie an explanation of one of the unusual features of the enclosure at High Island, its four entrances regularly spaced round the enclosing wall, the two landward ones having huts beside them, as if to regulate the entry of strangers. Perhaps these entrances were

18. Francoise Henry, *Irish Art in the Early Christian Period (to 800 A.D.)* (London: Methuen, 1965), p. 105, Pls. 34, 35.
19. Liam Prince. "Glencolumbkille, County Donegal, and its Early Christian Cross-slabs", *Journal of the Royal Society of Antiquaries of Ireland*, 71 (1941), 76-77.
20. Hugh Hencken, "Lagore Crannog. An Irish Royal Residence of 7th to 10th centuries A.D.", *Proceedings of the Royal Irish Academy*, 53C (1950), 129-30; Henry, *Irish Art*, Pl. 36.
21. Henry, *Irish Art*, Pl. 39.
22. Francoise Henry, "The Antiquities of Caher Island (Co Mayo)", *Journal of the Royal Society of Antiquaries of Ireland*, 77 (1947), 23-38.

designed to accommodate devotees following the prescribed order of such a *turas* in the sacred area at this western end of the island.

The shape of the monastic enclosure is neither rectilinear nor circular; it appears rather as an adaptation to its siting, tucked in under the scarped terrace to the east of it, encroaching in a straight line on the edge of the tiny lake to the south of it. Such adaptation of the shape of the monastic enclosure to the often rough and inhospitable terrain of the west is not unknown elsewhere: the hermitage on the Skellig rock in Kerry is really a series of roughly rectangular terraces,[23] and so is Killabuonia[24] on the mainland nearby. These rectilinear terraced outlines may also be evidence of an early tradition of Christian building in the west of Ireland in which the circular outline now so familiar elsewhere in both monastic and secular enclosures was not rigidly prescribed.

Wall-chambers like those at High Island are common features in secular and monastic buildings in the Celtic and Early Christian traditions of Ireland and Scotland. Staigue Fort in County Kerry is one famous example of such structures in a secular context.[25] An example in the monastic enclosure at Caher Island north of here has been documented by Dr Francoise Henry[22] (Fig. 7). If a functional rather than a traditional explanation of their presence is sought, then those in the hermitages might be regarded as places of penitential observance.

Carais Feichin fíal Fabhair,
nochar bé an crabadh breccach
docuiredh a asna truagh
le carcair cruaidh gan édach.[26]

This can be freely translated:

Generous Fechin of Fore loved this:
—It was no false piety—
He used lay his wretched body
In the stony cell without raiment.

23. Liam de Paor, "A Survey of Sceilg Mhichil", *Journal of the Royal Society of Antiquaries of Ireland*, 85 (1955), 174-87.
24. Henry, *Early Monasteries*, 102.
25. Séan P. O Riordáin, *Antiquities of the Irish Countryside* (London: Methuen, 1953), p. 7.
26. Whitley Stokes, "Cuimmin's Poem on the Saints of Ireland", *Zeitschrift fur Celtische Philologie*, 1 (1877), 59-73.

Although it appears that the oratory is often formally separated from the remainder of the monastic enclosure by an internal wall in sites like Inishmurray,[27] the inner rectangular enclosure completely surrounding the oratory at High Island is an unusual feature; only at Caher Island to the north can I find a similar feature[22] (Fig. 7). Both might have been built to create a processional way around the oratory, but the fact that we know so few examples among the many similar monasteries preserved along the west coast suggests that these are unique adaptations, possibly to the environment.

This inner enclosure may have been made necessary by the siting of the hermitage so close to the Atlantic storms; it was to protect the tiny community from the sea-spray or, more likely, from the gale gusts which might sweep infirm members across the open bawn of the monastery and into the lake or the ocean. The fact that there is evidence for a covered way linking the oratory's enclosure with the principal cell opposite its entrance may lend weight to this suggestion.

This unique inner enclosure, by surrounding the oratory and tomb, tends to mask the fact that, at the focus of the hermitage, there are three standard elements of the simple western monastery, cross-slab, oratory and saint's tomb, the first two visible today, the third attested by George Petrie's description of 1820. All three are present at Killabuonia[28] in Kerry, where the tomb is of the simple dog-kennel form well-known in Kerry and where the cross-slab stands between the tomb and the oratory (Fig. 8), cross and tomb ranged on the line of the west gable of the oratory. Two of the three can be seen, and the third presumed, at Loher,[29] south of Waterville, on the Skellig itself,[30] on Illaunloghan,[31] an island near Portmagee in Kerry, and at Caher Island.[22]

The arrangement of these three elements at the focal point of the monastery seems also to have been an ideal at the foundation of some early monasteries in the east of the country. At Clonmacnoise,[32] which was founded by Ciaran in 547 and grew over centuries into a very large enclosure having several churches,

27. W.F. Wakeman, *A Survey of the Antiquarian Remains on the Island of Inishmurray* (Dublin: Royal Society of Antiquaries of Ireland, 1893), p. 13.
28. Henry, *Early Monasteries*, 102.
29. ibid., 143.
30. de Paor, *Sceilg Mhichil*, fig. 3.
31. Henry, *Early Monasteries*, 97.
32. R.A.S. Macalister, *The Memorial Slabs of Clonmacnoise* (Dublin: Royal Society of Antiquaries of Ireland, 1909), pp. 141-42.

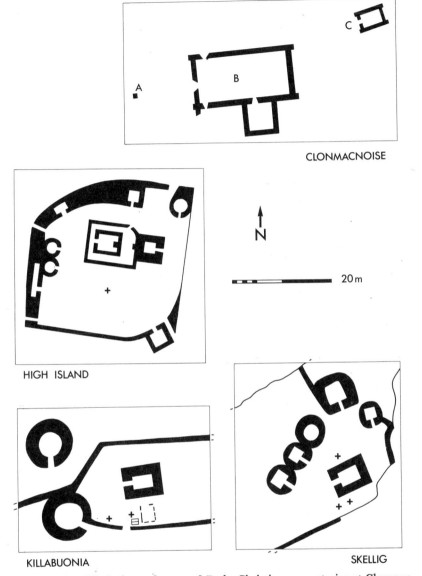

Fig. 8. Simplified plans of parts of Early Christian monasteries at Clonmacnoise, Co Offaly (after Macalister), High Island, Co Galway, Killabuonia and Skellig Mhichíl, Co Kerry (after Henry). The Cross of the Scriptures, the Cathedral and *Teampall Chiaráin* at Clonmacnoise are marked A, B and C respectively on the plan.

crosses and burials, a complex formed of these three elements can still be discerned on a terrace at the focal point of the enclosure (Fig. 8).

The present cathedral, which presumably stands on the site of the original church of the founder, has in front of its west entrance a High Cross erected about the year 908, the Cross of the Scriptures, on which the names of Colman, the abbot, and Flann, the king of Meath, are inscribed. This probably replaces an earlier cross-slab like those on High Island at this site. A short distance north-east of the church is the tiny *Teampall Chiaráin*, traditionally said to have been Ciaran's tomb, in which was found, early in the last century, the Crozier of the Abbots of Clonmacnoise, along with a number of other monastic relics. This building is thus a reliquary to house the bones and relics of the founder-saint, as is St Declan's House at Ardmore in Waterford and the Priests's House at Glendalough, both of quite late style; the analogue in Kerry is the simple dog-kennel shrine of sites like Killabuonia, Illaunloghan and Killoluaig,[33] where the saint's bones might be revered by touching them through a hole in the gable end of the tomb. Slane in County Meath has still the remains of one of these primitive shrines on the south side of the church.[34] The existence of such a primitive shrine in County Meath suggests that this type of tomb was widespread in the east of the country from the beginning of Christianity and that it was later replaced by more elaborate structures, as new fashions were adopted by monastic communities. Meanwhile, the west of the country adhered to the primitive ideal, retaining the simpler structures.

We have come a long way from High Island but it appears that the conjunction of oratory, cross-slab and founder's tomb was once common throughout the country, east and west, developing later into something more elaborate in the richer east, retaining its primitive cast in the ascetic and conservative west.

About the year 650, when Fechin came west from Fore in Westmeath and Cong in Mayo to the Atlantic at Omey and High Island, he may have been in retreat from a richer and more crowded east, seeking to achieve an asceticism of spirit in the austere and primitive environment of the west. He may even have recognised in the eastern monasteries latent or already developing signs of a trend towards worldliness: simple cross-slabs were soon to develop into elaborate High Crosses at Ahenny in the

33. Henry, *Early Monasteries*, 99.
34. RIA Ms. 3D6, p. 30 (du Noyer, *Antiquarian Sketches*).

Slievenamon area in the years about 700. It may be more than coincidence that Colman and his monks, leaving Lindisfarne in Northumbria after the synod of Whitby in 664, chose to set their Irish monastery on the Island of Inishbofin[35] only a few miles north of High Island.

35.   Kenney, *Sources*, p. 463.

Anthony Whilde

A Note on the Storm Petrel and Corncrake

The storm petrel (*Hydrobates pelagicus*) is Ireland's smallest and most delightful seabird. It is only six inches long and weighs little more than an ounce. Its sooty grey plumage and contrasting white rump give the impression of a house martin, but its black bill, with elongated tubular nostrils, place it firmly in the order of petrels which includes fulmars, shearwaters and albatrosses.

It is a bird which is rarely seen by laymen because it spends much of its time ranging over the open ocean and only stays on land for brief periods, usually on remote and inaccessible offshore islands. I was particularly pleased to find that this abundant but elusive creature had inspired Richard Murphy to write "Nocturne" and "Stormpetrel". In publishing these poems he will convey to many people, who would otherwise remain ignorant of these oceanic nomads, something of their interesting life style and a fragment of the pleasure to be had in studying them at close quarters.

"Gipsy of the sea" conjures up the picture of a wanderer, quartering the ocean and snatching sustenance where it can. But like a gipsy, our wanderer, the storm petrel, follows a fairly regular routine, albeit difficult for us to recognise. The autumn and winter months are spent gliding and fluttering a few inches above the heaving ocean, occasionally hovering, with feet pattering the surface, and picking up morsels from the sea surface. This behaviour gives the bird its name—after St Peter. In Irish he is known as *Peadairín na Stoirme*.

Sailors, ever superstitious, regarded the appearance of storm petrels close to the ship as an ill omen, accompanied as they were by storms. But petrels also have to return to land to breed, and this, no doubt, was in the mind of the sailor who carved his girl's name on a petrel's bill, hoping that it would carry ashore the tidings of his well-being to his loved one.

By late April or early May, mature petrels are returning to their breeding colonies on remote offshore islands, arriving with the afterglow of the setting sun and departing three or four hours later, before sunrise.

Mates of previous years probably meet up in the same burrows (there is no evidence to suggest that pairs stay together during the autumn and winter) that they occupied before and the ritual of producing a new generation is initiated. A storm petrel lays a single white egg in an earth burrow, in a hole amongst the boulders of a storm beach, in dry stone walls or in the remains of old buildings. On High Island the miner's hut and the ruins of St Feichin's monastery are the main breeding haunts, but a few pairs also breed at the holy well at the highest point of the island. And it is true that storm petrels breed in human skulls!

Occupied nest holes can often be identified by the musty smell emanating from them. This is produced by the uneaten remains of the oily, partly digested food which is fed to the chick by the parents. It is a clinging odour, and musty-smelling clothes are the penalty a careless researcher must pay for upsetting a fully laden petrel which can readily turn its powers of regurgitation to offensive purposes.

By midnight on a clear June night the "Pulse of the rock" can reach an impressive pitch as petrels sit "churring", some perhaps incubating eggs, in their spartan, rock-bound holes. This, "A song older than fossils", has been echoing since the Miocene epoch, over twenty million years ago. Since that time the storm petrel and the environment to which it has become so perfectly adapted have probably changed very little. Provided Man does not destroy its food supply in the sea or drive it away from its remote breeding haunts, its future is secure.

The west coast of Ireland is one of the main breeding stations of the storm petrel in the North Atlantic. The islands of Kerry, north Mayo and Donegal support the greatest numbers, perhaps in excess of 50,000 pairs. However, it is almost impossible to arrive at an accurate figure because of the nocturnal activity of the birds and the fact that many of those at the colonies, particularly in mid-summer, are highly mobile, young, non-breeding birds (storm petrels do not breed until they are five or six years old), perhaps 'sizing up' the situation for when they 'come of age'.

During the last two summers, with a number of colleagues, I have ringed about 500 storm petrels on High Island. This very limited research has suggested that many more than 500 petrels visit the island. Recaptures of ringed birds have illustrated the fidelity of storm petrels to their breeding sites, even after months away roaming the apparently featureless ocean.

*　　*　　*

In contrast to the storm petrel, the corncrake (*crex crex*) is probably known to most people, at least in Ireland, by the characteristic 'crekking' of males from April through to July or occasionally August. This harsh call, usually most noticeable at night, but also produced during the day, is sadly becoming scarcer, as earlier mechanised harvesting of hay and silage sweeps away adults, nests and young.

In Britain the corncrake is now a rare bird and is afforded special protection. In Ireland it is commoner but also declining, even in its last strongholds in the west where the scythe is still used to cut hay. Richard Murphy's "Song for a Corncrake" echoes the inevitable fate of this attractive but elusive species.

The name corncrake is something of a misnomer because the bird breeds in various types of tall vegetation from sedgy meadows to nettle beds. By far the commonest habitat in Britain and Ireland is fields of grass grown for hay or seed. Wet, marshy fields, occupied in parts of the Continent, are seldom used here, except in the west of Ireland.

Last spring there were three males 'crekking' in the fields around my house in west Galway, day and night, but, try as I might, I could not catch sight of any of them, nor could I locate a nest. As we are told in "Corncrake", they fly low and close to the vegetation, unlike most birds, and generally remain hidden from all but the luckiest observer.

The corncrake is with us only for the spring and summer, and in August it returns to its warmer wintering grounds in central, eastern and southern Africa. Some birds fly as far afield as Madagascar, while a few remain in southern Europe, the Mediterranean, and regions eastwards to Iran.

Jonathan Williams

A Glossary to *The Battle of Aughrim* and *The God Who Eats Corn*

The Battle of Aughrim and *The God Who Eats Corn* were published in one volume in 1968 by Faber and Faber. Unfortunately the book was allowed to go out-of-print in 1976. Both poems are included in *High Island. New and Selected Poems*, published by Harper and Row in 1974.

In the glossary, the sections of the poems are given in Roman numerals and the particular line numbers in Arabic numerals.

The Battle of Aughrim

I Now

1, 2 **eskar**

Or esker. Irish *eiscir*. A long, irregular ridge of gravel, sand and other alluvial deposits, which was once the bed of a river in the ice-sheet. This particular eskar extends in a half-circle to link up with the high ground of Urachree on the west side of the bog. It gave the Williamite forces access to the Irish right at the present Tristaun bridge. See also 'Before', 5, 40; 'After', 5, 15.

the drained bogs

The bogs were drained eastward during the nineteen sixties by streams flowing towards the Suck.

3 **credal**

Pertaining to a creed or religious belief. See 'After', 5, 16.

4 **Names in the rival churches are written on plaques**

There are two churches in Aughrim, one Catholic, the other Church of Ireland. There are no plaques in the Catholic church at least. The poet may be referring to names engraved on tombstones.

5 **defended with pikes**

"The second line [of the Jacobite infantry] stood in formed battalions, pikes behind the musketeers, and with intervals between the formations, about where the road runs." (G.A. Hayes-McCoy, *Irish Battles* (London:

Longmans, Green and Co Ltd, 1969), p. 251).

6 **a rood**
A plot of land, properly containing forty square poles or perches (a quarter of an acre). See 'Now', 7, 6.

7 **Morning fog**
See the Reverend George Story, *A Continuation of the Impartial History of the Wars of Ireland*, p. 126, for confirmation that the morning of the battle was foggy too.

8 **a stream passed by cavalry traitors**
The stream flows beside Aughrim Castle. The "traitors" were Brigadier Henry Luttrell and his superior, Major-General Dominick Sheldon. Luttrell was in charge of the first line of the Irish left wing: four regiments of horse and four of dragoons. His responsibility was to defend the causeway but, after a token resistance, he withdrew.

9-10 **A Celtic cross by the road commemorates no battle**
But someone killed in a car, Minister of Agriculture
"To the memory of Patrick Hogan TD, first Minister for Agriculture, Irish Free State, accidentally killed here 14 July 1936. May God have Mercy on his Soul." He was returning to his home at Kilrickle when his car swerved and struck the parapet of Aughrim bridge.

11 **the fast trunk-route**
The main Dublin to Galway road. This highway, bypassing Aughrim village, was built in the mid-nineteen sixties, when the poem was being written.

14 **the National School**
Where Martin Joyce was headmaster. He collected an impressive archive of relics from the battlefield, which were housed in the school while he taught there. See note to 'Before', 1, 2.

15 **Patrick Sarsfield's** *Would to God . . .*
Although historians are sceptical, "Would to God this wound had been for Ireland" were supposedly the last words of Patrick Sarsfield, who was mortally wounded at the Battle of Landen (also called Neerwinden) near Liège in Belgium on 19 July 1693 (old-style calendar). See 'After', 4, 50-51.

16 **Battle Hill**
Kilcommodan Hill, four or five miles south-west of Ballinasloe. The hill, which rises some 350 feet above the bog, stretches south-eastwards from the village. The Jacobite forces were on its eastern slope.

19 **the rector's glebe**
The land of the rector of the Church of Ireland. A glebe is a portion of land assigned to a clergyman as part of his ecclesiastical benefice.

22 **the death-cairn of St Ruth**
A heap of rough stones (Irish *carn*) and a blackthorn bush mark the spot where St Ruth is said to have been killed. The cairn is about 250 yards north-east of the fort which was used by the French general as his headquarters.

23 *Le jour est à nous, mes enfants*
See John T. Gilbert (ed.), *A Jacobite Narrative of the War in Ireland 1688-1691* (reprinted Shannon: Irish University Press, 1971), p. 141: "On the other side, general St Ruth, remarking the condition of the enemy and his own success, cried out in his language with joy: 'Le jour est à nous, mes enfants'." See 'During', 1, 47.

Gilbert's edition of part of the manuscript 'A Light to the Blind' is an important historical source, written about twenty years after the battle. It is known as the Plunkett manuscript.

2, 6 **the absentee**
A member of the landlord Ascendancy class who lived away from Ireland but who received incomes and pensions from estates in the country.

8 **penal master**
The Penal Laws, enacted by Irishmen through the predominantly Protestant parliament in Dublin, codified the underling status of Irish Catholics for most of the eighteenth century and gave security and power to the Protestant minority. A series of coercive measures introduced at the end of the seventeenth and beginning of the eighteenth centuries debarred Catholics from parliament, from holding government office, from entering the judiciary or legal profession, and from holding commissions in the army or navy. Catholics were forbidden to buy land or take long leases and there were similar prohibitions regarding their education. By the seventeen nineties most of the laws were repealed. See 'Now', 6, 15.

9 **Rapparees, whiteboys, volunteers, ribbonmen**
Lawless, Irish Catholic organisations or secret societies.
Rapparees (Irish *rapaire*, a short pike) were pikemen or irregular soldiers: "Those are such of the Irish as are not of

the army, but the Country people armed in a kind of an hostile manner with Half-Pikes and Skeins, and some with Scythes, or Musquets. For the Priests the last three or four years past would not allow an *Irish man* to come to Mass, without he brought at least his Rapparee along; that they say in Irish signifies an Half-stick, or a Broken-beam, being like an Half-pike . . ." (Reverend George Story, *An Impartial History of the Wars of Ireland*, p. 16). See 'Before', 9, 16; 'After', 4, 26.

The whiteboys were a Catholic peasant association which first appeared in Munster in the seventeen sixties. They wore white smocks over their clothing to distinguish each other at night. The movement was originally formed to contest the enclosure of common land, but their outrages were also a protest against rack-renting. They were suppressed in the later seventeen eighties.

Ribbonmen were members of the Ribbon Society, active from 1820 to 1870 and at its peak between 1835 and 1855. The Society's name was taken from the green ribbon worn as a badge by members. Initially a secret Catholic association in Ulster, set up to defend themselves against Orangemen, the movement spread south and by the eighteen thirties had become essentially agrarian. An Act to suppress the Society was passed in June 1871. See "Droit de Seigneur", 15-18.

13 **July the Twelfth**
Orange Day in Northern Ireland and the focus of Ulster Protestant iconography and loyalism. The day is celebrated as the anniversary of the Battle of the Boyne, although under the Julian, old-style calendar, it would have been fought on 1 July. The Gregorian, new-style calendar was introduced to the British Isles in January 1752. Aughrim was fought on 12 July (old-style) but the battle does not have the same talismanic significance as the Boyne for Ulster loyalists.

16 **A grey cathedral on the old gaol wall**
The Roman Catholic Cathedral in Galway was built between 1959 and 1965 on the site of the old jail. It cost nearly £1 million to build.

17 **Knock shrine**
A village in south-east County Mayo. The little church has become the greatest centre of pilgrimage in Ireland, being the site of apparitions on 21 August 1879. The parish

priest's housekeeper, Mary McLoughlin, saw what she took to be the Virgin Mary standing between St Joseph and St John, and a plinth on which stood the Lamb of God against a cross.

18 **John Kennedy's head**
Kennedy, President of the USA 1960-63, was revered by Irish Catholics.

3, 3 **trainbands**
Abbreviation of 'trained-bands'. Locally raised body of citizens or militia.

4 **fife**
A shrill-toned instrument like a flute, used chiefly to accompany the drum in martial music.

5 **Apprentices**
Thirteen apprentice boys closed the gates at Derry on 7 December 1688 (o.s.) against Lord Antrim's Catholic regiment. This was followed by a fifteen-week siege of the city by James II's army, 19 April–31 July 1689. The closing and opening of the gates are annually celebrated on 18 December and 12 August (Gregorian calendar). On the latter date, the Protestant Apprentice Boys clubs march around the city walls in triumph.

13 **Derry, oakwood of bright angels**
The Irish *doire* means oakwood. About 546 St Columba founded a monastery in an oak-grove that gave the city its name. Londonderry is the official name for the city, which was given to the London merchant companies in the reign of James I, although, as Conor Cruise O'Brien has said, whether you say Londonderry or Derry is not a Protestant /Catholic shibboleth.

4, 1-2 **the black diary deeds/Gossiped**
The controversy about Sir Roger Casement's notorious 'black' diaries has been a protracted one. Scholars disagree on whether the diaries, which bring into play the issue of his alleged homosexuality, are genuine or forged. Extracts from the diaries were clandestinely circulated by the British authorities at the time of Casement's trial and, later, while an appeal against his death sentence was pending.

2 **prison lime**
After his execution on 3 August 1916, Casement's bones were put in a lime pit within the walls of Pentonville Jail in London.

4 **Casement's skeleton is flying home**
In 1964, Casement's centenary year, the newly elected Labour government in Britain decided to allow Casement's remains to be brought to Ireland. They were flown to Dublin on 23 February 1965.

7-8 **Whose welcome gaoled him when a U-boat threw**
This rebel quixote soaked on Banna Strand
In 1916 Casement sailed from Germany to Ireland in a U-boat to warn Eoin MacNeill that his attempts to organise an Irish brigade from German prison camps to fight in the projected Easter Rising had not been successful. With two companions, Casement landed on Banna Strand in County Kerry on Good Friday, 21 April. While the others went off to Tralee, Casement remained at an old rath near the beach. He was arrested there by a sergeant and a constable who took him to Tralee police station.

11 **fathered nothing**
Casement did not marry and had no children.
the traitor's dock
Casement was hanged for treason against the British Crown. Formerly a Unionist and loyal subject of the Crown, who had been knighted in 1911 for his distinguished career in the British diplomatic service, he had become a Sinn Féiner and republican.

12 **Wolfe Tone**
Theobald Wolfe Tone (1763-98) was, like Casement, a Protestant patriot-martyr. He helped to organise the United Irishmen. See 'After', 3, 33.

13 **From gaol yard to the Liberator's tomb**
The coffin lay in state at Arbour Hill Prison. On 24 February, a bitterly cold day with showers of snow and sleet, it was taken to Glasnevin cemetery, where the 'Liberator', Daniel O'Connell (1775-1847), who secured emancipation for Irish Catholics in 1829, is also buried.

18 **High Mass**
Celebrated at the Pro-Cathedral.

18-19 **Rebels in silk hats now**
Exploit the grave with an old comrade's speech
Eamon de Valera, then President of the Republic and eighty-two years old, delivered the graveside oration. Since he had been ill, he was advised to cover his head. "Casement", he replied, "deserves better than that." Brian Inglis, *Roger Casement* (London: Hodder & Stoughton,

1973), p. 400.

5, 1-2   **a symposium**

On Ireland's Jacobite war

The Military History Society of Ireland held a dinner in Renmore Barracks, Galway on 10 June 1962. Earlier in the day, members had toured the city studying the part it had played in the Jacobite war.

5 **an imperial garrison**

Renmore was once the barracks of the old Connaught Rangers. Colonel, the Reverend Thomas Ormsby, the poet's maternal grandfather, was commissioned in the Connaught Rangers.

8 **'A Soldier's Song'**

The Irish national anthem: "*Seo dhibh, a cháirde, duan oglaigh*" (We'll sing a song, a soldier's song).

9 **One hands me**

Martin Joyce of Aughrim.

6, 3-4   **men had to row**

Five miles, twelve centuries ago

To Inishbofin, five miles from Cleggan, County Galway.

6 **monks' litany**

St Colman (c. 632-676) founded a monastery on Inishbofin in 664, after he had been defeated at the Synod of Whitby on the question of the date of Easter.

7 **stormed by viking raids**

The first Norse raids on Ireland occurred at the end of the eighth century and continued to the eleventh century.

9-10 **Pirates found it and roofed a fort**

A mile west, commanding the port

In the sixteenth century Inishbofin was in the hands of a pirate called Bosco. Little is known of this legendary figure but he is said to have had a blockhouse at the harbour mouth, known as Bosco's Castle. The present star fort was built by Cromwellians during the sixteen fifties and was used by them as a garrison post.

11 **Red-clawed choughs**

Red-legged crows which frequent coasts and islands in the West of Ireland. See "The Cleggan Disaster", 245-46; "Walking on Sunday", 12.

12 **Guards throw priests to the sea's jaw**

The Cromwellians took over Inishbofin in 1652 and used the island as a concentration camp for priests and monks captured on the mainland. They were thrown down on the rocks and it is said that a bishop was chained there and drowned.

13 James the Shit
James II (1633-1701) who reigned from 1685 to 1688. In Irish *Seamus a' Chaca*.

16 Hedge-scholars
The Penal Laws offered Catholic parents the choice of educating their children in Protestant schools or not at all. Catholics held schools in the open country and, by the end of the eighteenth century, these hedge-schools were the only providers of education for Catholics.

21 my garden path
In Cleggan.

22 lath
A narrow, thin strip of wood which is nailed to rafters to support slates or tiles.

7, 1 Cromwellian demesne
Demesne is a variant of *domain* and is commonly used in Ireland to mean an estate attached to a big house.

2 bronze age raths
Prehistoric Irish hillforts, comprising an enclosure, usually circular, made by a strong earthen wall. See 'Before', 5, 22.

3-4 a child fell dead the moon
Her father cut hawthorn in those weird rings
Fairies are said to hold the hawthorn tree sacred, and cutting hawthorn on a rath is considered to be fatal.

9 Gallipoli
Between April 1915 and January 1916, by commanding the Dardanelles waterway, Turkey was able to stop the Allies joining forces with Russia in the war against Germany, Austria-Hungary and Turkey.

11 Slate he stripped from a Church of Ireland steeple
· cf. 'Before', 10, 17-18.

18 obelisk
A tapering stone column.

20 'Gouldings Grows'
Gouldings Chemicals Ltd produces fertiliser.

8, 6 I'm three weeks old
The end of August 1927.

11 Fight the good fight
The name of a hymn by John S.B. Monsell (1811-75), son of the Archdeacon of Derry.

13 Under the Holy Table there's a horse's skull

One of the Millers, ancestors of the poet, had a favourite horse whose hoof was preserved in Milford House, near Kilmaine, County Mayo, Richard Murphy's boyhood home. According to the poet's brother, the horse's head had been buried in Kilmaine Church, underneath the Holy Table.

16 **The horse cantered the wounded master home**
See "The Woman of the House", 45-46.

17 **I'm saved from Rome**
He was baptised in the Church of Ireland at Kilmaine.

9, 12 **Has a beginning in my blood**
The poet's ancestors fought on both sides at Aughrim. Writing the poem helped him to unify the divisions within himself.

II Before

1, 2 **a teacher**
Martin Joyce of Aughrim, teacher, military historian and archivist. Richard Murphy derived a lot of lore about the . battle from him and the two became good friends.

3-4   **a poem**
Written in a language that has died
Irish is the language, but the reference is to an imaginary source and not to any specific poem. Many Irish poets have written of the battle in both Irish and English, including Seamas Dall MacCuarta, Thomas Moore and Emily Lawless.

11 **Aughrim, the horse's ridge**
The Irish *Eachdhrium* means Horse-hill.

14 **the colonist's advance**
On 11 July 1691 (o.s.), Baron Ginkel marched the Williamite forces westwards to Ballinasloe. He crossed the Suck early on the following morning and proceeded to Aughrim. His ultimate aim was to take Galway and Limerick from the Jacobites.

15 **Twenty thousand soldiers on each side**
The numbers have been variously stated by both participants and historians, but the consensus is that there were approximately 20,000 men in each army.

18 **a causeway two abreast could cross**
A narrow causeway, about sixty yards long, which led to Aughrim Castle and from which it was exposed to fire. See

the Plunkett manuscript, p. 138: ". . . an old broken causeway, only large enough for two horses to pass it at a time . . ."

21 **absent kings**
James II had left Ireland after his defeat at the Boyne and was in exile at St Germain-en-Laye near Paris. At the time of Aughrim, his son-in-law, William III, was in the Netherlands.

22 **basset table**
Basset was a gambling card game played in the eighteenth century.

24 **Decide if bread be God**
This underlines the religious nature of the war of the two kings. There was a theological disagreement about transubstantiation between Catholic and Protestant.

2, St Ruth's address is transcribed verbatim from Story's *A Continuation of the Impartial History*, pp. 123-25. It was supposedly found in the pocket of his dead secretary after the battle and may have been forged.

The Reverend George Story was an English chaplain who arrived in Ireland in August 1689 and served with the Williamite army while the war lasted. He was appointed Dean of Connor in December 1694 and was made Dean of Limerick in April 1705. He died in 1721.

3, 1 **Teigue**
An English transcription of the Irish *Tadhg*, commonly used as a nickname for an Irishman. Loyalists in Ulster use the term to identify a Catholic.

7 **Sarsfield's troop**
He commanded a regiment of horse at the battle.

4, The poet probably derived this section from an incident described by Story, *An Impartial History*, p. 71:
"On *Saturday* morning the 29th [June 1690] there hap'ned an *Irish* Man and a Woman to be near a Well that was by the King's Tent, they had got something about them which the Soldiers believed was Poyson, to spoil the Waters, and to destroy the King and His Army: this spread presently abroad, and a great many Soldiers flocked about them, they were immediately both Judges and Executioners, hanged the Woman, and almost cut the Man in pieces."

5, 1 **Kelly's land**
The incidents set down in this section and in section 2 of

'During' are a strong tradition in the Aughrim area. It is said that the renegade sheep farmer called O'Kelly lived in Kilcloony parish, about a mile north of the battlefield.

4 **Mullen the herd**
Also remembered in local lore.

8 **cuirass**
A piece of iron or brass armour, reaching down to the waist and consisting of a breast-plate and back-plate fastened together. It was musket-proof and was often worn by cavalry.

9 **tucks**
Principally Scottish dialect, to describe the tapping or soft beating of a drum.

10 **Buff-coated**
On the record of the poem, produced by Claddagh Records, this becomes "green-coated". Most of the uniforms in the Jacobite army were red, with either orange or white.

17 **bivouacs**
A temporary encampment. The Jacobite camp extended across the top of the ridge and probably along its western slope.

22 **Up hill through hedgegaps to an ancient rath**
On St Ruth's instructions, the hedges on the hillside were cut into enclosures to enable the infantry to take up sheltered positions behind the low field boundaries and so retreat speedily in the ditches. The hill fortress used by St Ruth as his headquarters is at the top of Kilcommodan hill.

24 **Bourbon lilies**
The fleur-de-lis was adopted very early by French kings as their royal emblem.

36 **my honour**
Which he had to salvage after losing Athlone.

38 **St Ruth's**
Lieutenant General Charles Chalmont, Marquis of St Ruth. Before he came to Ireland, he had a distinguished military career in the French army and served in the wars in Holland, Flanders and Germany. He was made a Lieutenant General in 1688 and in 1691 replaced the Duke of Berwick as General of James's army in Ireland. He arrived in Ireland on 9 May 1691.
'Foutez-moi le camp!'

Foutre le camp means to scram, to do a bunk.

39 **halberds**
A halberd is a battle-axe and pike at the end of a long staff.

40 **river Suck**
Rises in a small lake seven miles west of Castlerea, County Roscommon, and flows sixty miles south-south-east along the Roscommon-Galway border, past Ballinasloe, to connect with the Shannon at Shannonbridge.

44 **casques of shot**
This is puzzling since 'casques' are helmets. The sense here is barrels, or *casks*, of shot.

46 **Danish mercenaries**
Ginkel had six battalions of Danish infantry and three regiments of horse. Mercenaries, hired from Denmark by a treaty in September 1689, fought at the Boyne. The German Duke of Wurtemberg-Neustadt, the leader of the Danish mercenary force, was Ginkel's second-in-command at Aughrim.

47 **hogweed**
Cow-parsnip, a common weed of hedgerows and open woodland.

49 **a grey house**
Probably belonging to Frederick Trench, a Huguenot, who gave his house at Garbally (between Aughrim and Ballinasloe) as a hospital for the Williamite forces.

49-50 **the Dutch/Commander**
Lieutenant-General Ginkel. Godart van Reede Ginkel (1630-1703) was born and died at Utrecht. He followed William to England in 1688, commanded a body of horse at the Boyne and was active at the siege of Limerick. In September 1690 he was given sole charge of the forces in Ireland and remained in command for the rest of the war. He received the earldom of Athlone in 1692 and the barony of Aughrim.

53 **Finch**
Most contemporary sources identify the gunner as Trench, an experienced artillery officer.

6, 2 **matchlocks**
Muskets. A match was placed in the gun lock to ignite the powder.

8-9 **Who cares which foreign king**
Governs, we'll still fork dung

Daniel Hoffman (in *Poetry*, 114, August 1969) has pointed out how these lines echo Yeats's "Parnell" couplet:
"Parnell came down the road, he said to a cheering man: 'Ireland shall get her freedom and you still break stone'."

7, 6 **St Brigid's well**
St Brigid, with St Patrick and St Columcille, is one of Ireland's patron saints.

    7 **our friary bells**
Probably Kilconnell Friary, about four miles north-west of Aughrim.

    8 **the tide of psalms flooding the plain**
The psalms came from Ginkel's Protestant army. Mass was celebrated in the Jacobite camp on the morning of the battle, a Sunday. Macaulay says "In every regiment priests were praying, shriving, holding up the host and the cup." (*History of England From the Accession of James II*, London: J.M. Dent, Everyman Edition, Vol. III, p. 333).

  10 **your man**
A very common Irish idiom.

8, 1 **God was eaten in secret places**
Surreptitious celebration of the Eucharist by Catholics.

9, 3 **The painted warts of Cromwell**
cf. "Droit de Seigneur", 4.

    6 **the king's head**
King Charles I was executed outside the Banqueting House in Whitehall on 30 January 1659. The poet can trace his ancestry, through an illegitimate line, to Charles Stuart.

  13 **my daughter**
The voice and home is of Robert Miller, an ancestor of the poet's mother, who lived in Ballycushin, about six miles from Tuam in County Galway.

  14 **Sefauchi's Farewell**
A piece for harpsichord by Henry Purcell (c. 1659-95). The air refers to the departure from England of Sefauchi (Giovanni Francesco Grossi, 1653-97), an Italian male soprano, who for a time was attached to the chapel of James II.

  27 **Red-mouthed O'Donnell**
Hugh Balldearg O'Donnell. ('Balldearg' means 'of the red spot'.) O'Donnell, born in County Donegal, was descended from the family of the old Earl of Tyrconnell in Ulster. For many years he served in the Spanish army and had commanded an Irish regiment there. He returned to

Ireland a few days after the Boyne, and at the time of Aughrim claimed that he and his horde of a thousand Ulstermen had orders from St Ruth to burn or garrison castles and houses. Tradition says that Robert Miller entertained O'Donnell while his troops were far from the battlefield. Before Sligo was besieged, O'Donnell made terms with Ginkel and abandoned the Jacobites. Eventually he returned to Spain and was reinstated in the army. He died in 1704.

33-34 **a wine-blotted birth-mark/Of prophecy**
It was a familiar belief that the true Earl of Tyrconnell, marked on his body with a red spot, would come from abroad into Ireland, "and do there great matters for his country". (Plunkett MS, p. 151).

10,1-9 Story describes an encounter with rapparees:
"The rest escaped to the Bogs, and in a moment all disappeared, which may seem strange to those that have not seen it, but something of this kind I have seen myself; and those of this Party assured me, that after the Action was over, some of them looking about amongst the Dead, found one *Dun* a Serjeant of the Enemies, who was lying like an Otter, all under Water in a running Brook, (except the top of his Nose and his Mouth. . . ." (*An Impartial History*, p. 152).

18 **snipe**
Game birds which frequent boggy marshes. The whirring noise is produced by the beating of their wings. See "The Reading Lesson", 10.

20 **nightjar**
A greyish-brown, well-camouflaged bird, which hunts at night. See "The Glass Dump Road", 9.

III During

1, 4 **King's Life Guards**
A royal regiment of the household cavalry, first raised by Charles II in Flanders in 1656. The first squadron accompanied St Ruth at Aughrim.

8-9 **to put/The kingdom upon a fair combat**
The phrase is in the Plunkett MS: "so he [St Ruth] chose to put the kingdom upon a fair combat, being unalterably resolved to bury his body in Ireland or regain it speedily." (p. 137).

11 **Losing Athlone**
These lines also echo Plunkett. St Ruth failed to reinforce the troops in the Irish part of Athlone town, which was taken by Ginkel on 30 June 1691 (o.s.).

12 **his Most Christian master**
Louis XIV (1638-1715), James II's cousin. The Plunkett MS refers to him in like terms: "The most Christian king", "his most Christian majesty".

17-18 **In ranks below colonel**
His army only speaks Irish
Not literally true.

24 **Prince of Condé's**
Henry Jules de Bourbon (1643-1709), fifth Prince of Condé, who served in many military campaigns from 1666 to 1693.

30 **A wife-tormentor's**
He was apparently an incorrigible wife-beater. See *The Memoirs of the Duke of Saint-Simon*, trans. Bayle St John (London: Samuel Bagster & Sons Ltd, 1901), Vol. II, p. 313.

34-35 **the sulphurous/Agony of Huguenots**
Macaulay attests to St Ruth's cruelty: "In his own country he was celebrated as the most merciless persecutor that had ever dragooned the Huguenots to mass." (p. 325). Story, too, mentions him as "one of the greatest Persecutors of the Protestants in *France*." (p. 134).

40 **He rides downhill**
Both Story and the Plunkett MS corroborate this.

44 **The time is near sunset**
Charles O'Kelly, in *Macariae Excidium, or The Destruction of Cyrus* (a contemporary Catholic account of the war), sets the time "about sunset"—probably between eight and nine o'clock.

2, 3 **the cannon**
G.A. Hayes-McCoy places the cannon in a battery south-west of Caltragh fort, a half-mile south of Melehan bridge. The six-pounder was preserved in the armoury of Dublin Castle until the end of the eighteenth century.

4 **The victory charge**
Contemporary historians maintain that St Ruth had resolved to advance his cavalry, oppose the enemy at the causeway, and make his victory complete.

6 **galloped towards the setting sun**

Tradition alleges that St Ruth was buried in Kilconnell Friary, but Loughrea, fourteen miles to the south-west, is the more credible place of his burial.

8 **the sun's rod tipped the altar hill**
For a similar image, see "Sailing to an Island", 14.

3, 2 **his regiment**
G.A. Hayes-McCoy writes that the "cavalry of the right wing, a troop of the Life Guard, three regiments of horse and more dragoons, was apparently commanded by Sarsfield." (p. 250).

6 **white cockade**
A knot of ribbons or a rosette, worn in the hat as a badge of office. It takes its name from the cock's comb and was worn by followers of Charles Edward, the Young Pretender. See 'After', 4, 49.

7 **skirls**
This word, probably of Scandinavian origin, is used to describe the bagpipe's shrill, screaming sound.

9 **When King James had run**
After his defeat he fled to Dublin. From there he rode to Duncannon on Waterford Harbour, took a boat for Kinsale and then sailed for France.

10 **the Dutch usurper's**
William III was the posthumous son of William II of Orange and Mary, eldest daughter of Charles I of England. He married his cousin Mary, daughter of James II by Anne Hyde, in 1677. They were proclaimed King and Queen of England on 13 February 1689.

12 **Ballyneety**
On 12 August 1690, at this village just to the south-east of Limerick, Sarsfield and his troopers made a daring raid on a Williamite siege-train coming from Dublin with battering-cannon, ammunition and provisions. He surprised the wagon-train at night-time.

13 **Earl of Lucan**
For his action at Ballyneety, the Duke of Tyrconnell recommended Sarsfield to King James's favour. In January 1691 Tyrconnell returned from France and brought the news that Sarsfield had been given the earldom of Lucan.

14 **Commands the reserve**
Historians have disagreed about Sarsfield's exact position on the battlefield. Macaulay places him in charge of the reserve. G.A. Hayes-McCoy concludes that "the

happenings of the last phase of the struggle do much to confirm the statement that he commanded the augmented cavalry force on the right wing." (p. 268).

15 **saviour of Limerick**
Because of his bravery at Ballyneety.

15-16 **knows/Nothing of St Ruth's plan**
Irish nationalist historians blame St Ruth for keeping his battle plan secret. They claim that, had he divulged it to his fellow officers, the Jacobite victory would have been secure after his death.

20-21 **The order to wait for further Orders behind the hill**
Captain Robert Parker, who fought for William at Aughrim, wrote that St Ruth gave Sarsfield "positive directions not to stir from thence his post until he received his orders." (Parker's *Memoirs* were published in Dublin in 1746). See 'After', 4, 31-32.

23 **Throwing away muskets**
Story (*A Continuation*, p. 148) writes that Ginkel gave sixpence apiece for muskets thrown away by the enemy. So many were handed in that the price was cut to twopence.

4, 5-6 **The wrong kegs of ball were consigned to the castle**
Aughrim Castle (just north of the village) and the walls and ditches around it were occupied by Colonel Walter Burke's regiment. They fought with French muskets, the bore of which was smaller than that of the standard English arms. Their reserve ammunition contained English musket balls which were too big for their muskets and therefore useless. See the Plunkett MS, p. 147.

11-12 **they loaded muskets with tunic buttons**
J.G. Simms says that this embellishment of the musket-balls story did not get into the records until fifty years after the battle. Although it is not possible to verify the story, it would be facile to dismiss it. See P.K. Egan, *The Parish of Ballinasloe* (1960).

15 **Crossed the causeway**
Ruvigny, the Huguenot cavalry commander, led the way across.

19 **They fell with no quarter**
The evidence appears to belie this. Story says that Colonel

Burke, his major, eleven other officers and forty men surrendered and were taken prisoner. (*A Continuation*, p. 136).

5, 1 **Luttrell**
Brigadier Henry Luttrell (1655?-1717), whose regiments of horse were on the Irish left. See 'After', 3.

3 **beanfield**
Gort na Bpónaire or Bainfield is a townland of Aughrim.

11 **priding cavalry**
The Plunkett MS is vehemently critical of the withdrawal and treachery of the commanding officers of the Jacobite left: "And so let them keep their priding cavalry to stop bottles with." (p. 146).

13 **Ten miles to a dinner**
Martin Joyce thinks that this might be at Mr Mason's house in Loughrea.

6, 1 **the retreat**
Sarsfield and Viscount Galmoy covered the retreat of the survivors. The cavalry rode to Loughrea and Portumna, and thence to Limerick.

IV After
1, 1 **A wolfhound sits**
Story (*A Continuation*, p. 147) is probably the source for this section: "And there is a true and remarkable Story of a Greyhound belonging to an *Irish* Officer: the Gentleman was killed and stript in the Battle, whose Body the Dog remained by night and day; and tho he fed upon other Corps with the rest of the Dogs, yet he would not allow them or any thing else to touch his Master. When all the Corps were consumed, the other Dogs departed, but this used to go in the Night to the adjacent Villages for Food, and presently to return again to the place where his Masters Bones were only then left: and thus he continued till *January* following when one of Col. *Foulks*'s Soldiers being quartered nigh hand, and going that way by chance, the Dog fearing he came to disturb his masters Bones, flew upon the Soldier: who being surprized at the suddenness of the thing, unslung his Piece, then upon his back, and killed the poor Dog."
A wolfhound is a native Irish dog of enormous size and heraldic appearance.

2 **ensign's**
A commissioned officer in the infantry. Originally the soldier who carried the ensign.

6 **Prisoners are sabred**
Many thousands on the Jacobite side were massacred. Yet nearly 500 prisoners were taken. The Williamite dead were buried.

10 **six thousand skulls**
According to the historians, an accurate figure. The Jacobites lost about 4,000 men and the Williamite casualties were close to 2,000.

17 **rowan tree**
Another name for the mountain ash. See line 1 above.

18 **The wild geese**
Irish emigré soldiers of fortune. In the eighteenth century those who left Ireland to join the brigades in France and Spain were called wild geese, supposedly because they were so entered in the ships' manifests.

20 **keens**
Irish *caoin*, to mourn and wail for the dead.

21 **redcoat**
Specifically, a soldier in the British army.

26 **papistical**
Pertaining to the Pope and the doctrines of the Church of Rome.

2, This section is drawn from Story. For the most part, the words are not directly transcribed nor set down sequentially, but are selected and refracted by the poet. Lines 1-11 are taken from Story, *A Continuation*, p. 134, lines 26-35 from p. 325.

3, 1 **Luttrellstown**
The Luttrell's family estates were two miles north-east of Lucan, County Dublin, on the River Liffey. Henry Luttrell retired there after the death of William in 1702.

6 **Up torchlit quays from a coffee shop**
From Lucas's coffee shop on Cork Hill, Dublin, and then along the Liffey.

16-18 **pebbles**
Which he used at Mass in straw-roofed chapels
To lob at little girls
John Cornelius O'Callaghan in his *History of the Irish Brigades in the Service of France* (1840), p. 103, writes that he was told this about 1839 from "an intelligent

peasant" whose grandmother passed on the legend to him. The pebbles were cast to attract the attention of "every well-looking female of the lower orders, whether other men's wives, or not."

19 **town house**
In Stafford Street, Dublin, now Wolfe Tone Street.

21 **plunked**
Dropped suddenly and with a thud. A dialect word.

24 **Twenty-six years ago**
Henry Luttrell was shot on 21 October 1717 (o.s.) and died the next day.

29-30 **the Duke of Bolton**
Offered three hundred pounds' reward
Charles Paulet (1661-1722), Lord Lieutenant of Ireland 1717-21, and the Duke of Bolton. The money was offered to anyone who could apprehend the assassin but nobody came forward. The Irish House of Commons declared that there was reason to believe that the act was one of revenge by the papists.

36 **smashed the skull with a pickaxe**
"The peasant . . . likewise told me that, towards the end of the last century, Henry Luttrell's tomb, near Luttrellstown, was broken open at night by some of the peasantry of the neighbourhood, and his skull taken out, and smashed with a pick-axe . . ." (O'Callaghan, *History of the Irish Brigades*, p. 104).

4, 1 **great-uncle in the portrait's grime**
Sarsfield was the great-uncle of Lady Bingham (born Anne Vesey of Lucan). The portrait, formerly in the possession of Sir Charles Bingham, Castlebar, County Mayo, forms the frontispiece to John T. Gilbert's edition of *The Jacobite Narrative of the War in Ireland 1688-1691*, op. cit.

The poet also claims descent from Patrick Sarsfield's brother, William, who married Mary Crofts, the sister of the Duke of Monmouth.

2 **Your emigration**
The Treaty of Limerick (3 October 1691) granted free transport to France for any soldier who desired it.

3 **racked**
To rack-rent or raise the rent of land above a normal and fair amount.

9 **Sedgemoor**
Sarsfield was wounded at the Battle of Sedgemoor, fought

on 6 July 1685. He was unhorsed while charging at the head of his troops. He fought for James II, whose men, under the Duke of Feversham, defeated the untrained and primitively armed rebels of the Duke of Monmouth.

10 **Monmouth**
James, Duke of Monmouth (1649-85), son of Lucy Walters and the first born of Charles II's many illegitimate children, was the Protestant champion and claimant to the throne after his father's death in February 1685. He came to England from the Netherlands in the summer of that year. Monmouth was captured while fleeing from the battlefield and was beheaded at the Tower of London on 15 July 1685.

14 **divine perfidious monarch's rout**
James's flight from Ireland after the Boyne was regarded by many of his followers as a breach of faith.

17 **At Limerick besieged**
Sarsfield was the mainstay of the resistance at Limerick in 1690. He opposed Tyrconnell's decision to surrender the city.

18 **'If this had failed, I would have gone to France'**
Story recounts (*An Impartial History*, p. 121) how the Irish took only one prisoner after Ballyneety. Sarsfield treated him civilly and told him "if he had not succeeded in that Enterprise, he had gone to *France*."

21 **A French Duke**
Antonin de Caumont, Comte de Lauzun, who reputedly said: "It is unnecessary for the English to bring cannon against such a place as this. What you call ramparts might be battered down with roasted apples." His opinion supposedly encouraged William to believe that a bold assault might induce Tyrconnell to surrender.

24 **lost your own estate**
In Lucan, County Dublin. O'Callaghan asserts that Sarsfield not only forfeited his estates but "good prospects of advancement" from William.

27-28 **blew his train/Of cannon skywards**
At Ballyneety, Sarsfield and his cavalry stuffed the guns with powder, fixed their mouths to the ground and then blew them up.

35 **you assumed command**
Sarsfield was prominent in the resistance at Limerick in September 1691 and took a leading part in the

negotiations which led to the Treaty.

36 **exile in your courteous conqueror's boat**
Sarsfield was with the final detachment which left Cork for France on 22 December 1691.

37 **'Change kings with us, and we will fight again'**
Gilbert Burnet, *History of His Own Time* (edition of 1823), Vol IV, p. 140.

38 **ten thousand men**
Plunkett puts the figure at 12,000 and some sources as high as 14,000. The figure of ten thousand included 4,000 women, children and old men. (See J.G. Simms, *Jacobite Ireland 1685-91* (London: Routledge & Kegan Paul, 1969), p. 259.

39 **women clutched the hawsers in your wake**
Story describes the harrowing scenes at the waterside: ". . . many of the Women . . . catching hold to be carried on Board, were dragged off, and through fearfulness, losing their hold, were drowned; but others who held faster had their fingers cut off, and so perished in sight of their Husbands, or Relations . . ." (*A Continuation*, p. 292).

41 **to come home stronger**
Sarsfield persuaded many soldiers to depart with him for France and guaranteed that they would return the following year with a strong army.

45 **Berwick the bastard**
James FitzJames Berwick (1670-1734), first Duke of Berwick, was the son of Arabella Churchill (sister of the future Duke of Marlborough) and James, Duke of York (later James II). For a time in 1690, when Tyrconnell was in France, Berwick was Governor General of Ireland. He himself left for France in February 1691.

46 **no head but grit**
Berwick described Sarsfield as "a man of an amazing stature, utterly devoid of sense, very good-natured and very brave." (Simms, op. cit., p. 158).

47 **your widow Honor for his wife**
Lady Honora de Burgh, second daughter of William, seventh Earl of Clanricarde, married Berwick in 1695, and died in 1698. They had one son. She and Sarsfield had a son, James, who inherited his father's title, and a daughter.

48 **the Sun King**
Louis XIV was known as 'Le Roi Soleil' because of the brilliance and pageantry of his court at Versailles.

lost your life
At the Battle of Landen, the French, under the Duc de
Luxembourg, defeated the Dutch-English army of William
III. Berwick was taken prisoner at the battle.

5,   3 the sheepwalk
See 'Before', 5, 9.

4 the great hunger and the exodus
During the famine of 1845-49, about a million Irish people
died of starvation and fever. Another million emigrated,
bearing disease to Britain and the New World.

13 the navel of an island
Aughrim is close to the 'geographical centre' of Ireland,
and, for the poet, the nexus of religious, historical and
cultural preoccupations.

20 houseled
To housel is to administer or receive the Eucharist.

21 dun
The ring-fort in Kilcommodan hill, known as Gleann na
Fola. See 'Before', 5, 22.

The God Who Eats Corn

I   1 Horace's farm
Horace (65 BC–8 BC), the Roman lyric poet and satirist,
was given a small farm by his patron Maecenus about 34
BC. It was in the Sabine hills, about fifteen miles north-
east of Tibur, and a place of great natural beauty and
tranquillity.

3 msasa
One of the most common and characteristic of the
woodland or savannah trees of tropical Africa. It has a
rough bark and a flattish crown. The leaves are deciduous
and vary in colour.

7 piccanin
Usually 'piccaninny'. It is used of the male child of black-
skinned southern Africans and is derived from the Spanish
pequeno (small).

8 **Queen Mother's cypress**
Queen Elizabeth, the Queen Mother, visited Rhodesia in 1953, to mark the centenary of the birth of Cecil Rhodes (5 July), and in 1957.

12 **Llewellin**
Lord Llewellin (John Jestyn Llewellin, 1893-1957), a former member of the British House of Lords who, in September 1953, became the first Governor-General of the Federation of Rhodesia and Nyasaland.

Tredgold
Sir Robert Clarkson Tredgold (b. 1899), a noted liberal, who was Chief Justice of both Southern Rhodesia and the Federation during the nineteen fifties. He resigned in 1960 over the Law and Order Maintenance Bill, whose oppressive provisions he found objectionable. He acted as Governor of Southern Rhodesia and as Governor General of the Federation on a number of occasions, and assumed the latter post on the death of Lord Llewellin in January 1957.

13 **Livingstone's heir**
For Livingstone, see III, 2

15 **boomslang**
Afrikaans for 'tree-snake', but it is applied to a particular tree-dwelling African snake, coloured bright green, sometimes with black patches. The boomslang glides along branches with exceptional speed and is very poisonous.

17 **candelabra**
A white-flowered evergreen with a palm-like stem and a crown of dense, spreading branches. Its green stems produce a milky juice when pierced.

21 **Cos**
The second largest of the Dodecanese islands, off the west coast of Greece in the S.E. Aegean Sea.

22 **shade where Hippocrates swore his oath**
Popular tradition associates the enormous plane-tree in the island's capital (also called Cos) with Hippocrates (c. 460 BC—c. 380 BC), the Greek physician. The tree has a circumference of thirty feet and its gigantic branches have to be supported by pillars.

Hippocrates, regarded as the founder of modern medicine, wrote a number of medical works known as the *Hippocratic Collection*, in which is found the *Hippocratic Oath*, a code of medical ethics which refers to the confidentiality of a doctor's consultation with his patients.

23 **voodoo**
An amalgam of beliefs and practices—including super-stition, sorcery and black magic—derived from African rites and the Christian faith. Its etymology has been variously defined: Richard Burton, the explorer, said that it was derived from *vodun*, a dialect form of the Ashanti word *obosum* (demon or fetish).

24 **trekkers**
People who migrate or go on a journey, usually by ox-wagon. From the Afrikaans *trekken*, to travel.

25 **indaba**
The poet himself glosses this Zulu word for a conference or parley between chiefs and headmen. See also III, 6; VI, 24.

II 3 **ibis**
A large, long-legged wading bird which is found in most of central Africa. Its feathers are white (adult birds have a black head and tail) and it has a slender down-curved bill. The ibis was worshipped by the Egyptians who ascribed magic powers to the bird.

4 **Rain-birds**
A common name for a number of birds of the *Cuculidae* family whose noisy cries are popularly believed to augur rain.

5 **pangas**
Long, broad-bladed, and sometimes hooked, knives. They resemble machetes and are used to cut brush, cane and logs.

9 **Hunkered**
Squatting on one's haunches.
kaffir
From the Arabic *kafir*, an infidel. A name once used by the Europeans of southern Africa to denote members of the Bantu peoples. It is now regarded as a term of abuse.

10 **rickety**
Suffering from rickets—a softening of the bones, especially in children, which results in bow-legs and emaciation.

14 **Clacking**
Chattering, clattering. The poet seems to be fond of this

echoic word: see "Seals at High Island", 4; "The Travelling Player", 7.

18 **tulip-trees**
Tall trees of the magnolia family. They have large greenish-yellow, tulip-shaped blossoms and soft white wood.

19 **booms**
Rapid expansion of economic activity.

24 **his father**
Canon R.W. Murphy of Ballinlough, County Roscommon and Clifden, County Galway. William Lindsay Murphy was born in Ballinlough on 4 May 1887.

III 2 **Livingstone's**
David Livingstone (1813-73), Scottish missionary and explorer, who came to Africa in 1841 and stayed for thirty years, returning home only twice. He discovered the Victoria Falls, the source of the Congo River, and made the first authenticated European crossing of the Continent.

the Founder's dream
Cecil John Rhodes (1853-1902), Cape Colony settler, politician and mining magnate. He was the son of an English parson and emigrated to South Africa in 1870. The Rhodesian territories were named after him and it was largely through his efforts that the area came under British dominion.

When in Kimberley, Rhodes planted his hand on a map of Africa and declared, "All this to be painted red; that is my dream."

3 **the Pioneer Column**
Rhodes's British South Africa Company was chartered by the British government in October 1889 and was thus enabled to administer the territories where it operated north of Bechuanaland. Attracted by the goldfields of Mashonaland, the Company formed a Pioneer Corps and recruited nearly 200 men who would be paid 7/6 a day and at the end of the trek were to receive 3,000 acres of land and the right to fifteen gold claims. An armed escort was necessary and was provided by 500 men of the newly formed BSAC police force. The Pioneer Column (the Corps and the police) began their 400-mile march at the end of June 1890. They built forts *en route* and on 13 September planted the Union Jack at a point in Mashonaland which

they called Fort Salisbury, after the British Prime Minister. After this formal occupation of the territory now known as Rhodesia, the Column demobilised to take up the mining claims and farms which they had been given.

4 **a childless millionaire**
Rhodes made his fortune in the diamond fields of Kimberley during the eighteen seventies and eighties. By 1888 he had acquired a monopoly in the diamond industry and had also taken a huge stake in the new goldfields on the Rand. He died unmarried.

5 **claiming a treaty**
On 11 February 1888 Lobengula, the King of the Matabele, signed a treaty of peace and amity with Queen Victoria. Later, Rhodes's envoys secured the exclusive rights to all metals and minerals in the King's domain (see note on line 8).

6 **the king's kraal**
Lobengula (c. 1832-94) became ruler of the Matabele in 1870.
A kraal is a colonial Dutch word for a village consisting of a collection of huts surrounded by a fence or stockade (the Spanish word *corral* is derived from it). The royal kraal was at Gubulawayo.

8 **the chameleon swallowed the black fly**
At the time when Rhodes's agents were negotiating with Lobengula to obtain his assent to an arrangement which would give Rhodes the exclusive right to mine gold in Mashonaland, the Matabele chief is reported to have made a striking remark to the Reverend C.D. Helm, the interpreter. It was quoted in a dispatch of Sir Sidney Shippard, the Administrator of Bechuanaland, who was in Gubulawayo: "Did you ever see a chameleon catch a fly? The chameleon gets behind the fly and remains motionless for some time, then he advances very slowly and gently, first putting forward one leg and then another. At last, when well within reach, he darts his tongue and the fly disappears. England is the chameleon and I am that fly." The day after the dispatch was written, Lobengula signed the concession, on 30 October 1888.

9 **dorps**
Dutch for a small town or village.

14-15 **Racial partners/Do not mix in wedlock sons and daughters**
The Federation of Rhodesia and Nyasaland, sired by the

white settler politicians, was a political instrument to entrench white superiority and maintain the subservience of the black people. As the poet says in his introductory note, partnership was a "myth". Most politicians believed in the segregation of black and white and their separate development, and would not countenance intermarriage or majority rule.

16 **The white man rides: the black man is his horse**
"Partnership between black and white in Central Africa is the partnership between the horse and its rider"—a remark commonly attributed to Sir Godfrey Martin Huggins, 1st Viscount Malvern (1883-1971), who was Prime Minister of Southern Rhodesia (1933-53) and first Prime Minister of the Federation (1953-56). Huggins was an apostle of white hegemony and made many other insulting remarks about the black people of Rhodesia.

21 **millet**
Cereal grass which bears a crop of small nutritious seeds.

IV 1 **white gods**
One of the books which Richard Murphy read before writing this poem was Ndabaningi Sithole's *African Nationalism* (first published by Oxford University Press, Cape Town, 1959). In chapter 17, "The Cracked Myth", the Reverend Sithole describes how the Matabele, the brave and warlike tribe which broke away from the Zulu nation, "called the white people *'Omlimu abadla amabele'*. – the gods that eat corn." According to the Matabele philosophy, anything that eats corn dies. The chapter explains how the white man in Africa gradually became stripped of his god-like aspects.

4 **sandveld**
See veld, IV, 30.

6 **mambas**
From the Zulu *imamba*. Tropical and southern African venomous snakes, related to the cobras but with no dilatable hood. There is a black and a green species.

8 **spoor**
Afrikaans for the track or footprint of an animal, particularly of a wild animal pursued as game.

9 **Governor's helmet**
William Lindsay Murphy was Governor of the Bahamas

from 1945 to 1949 when he retired. He was acting Governor of Southern Rhodesia in 1954 and acting Governor General of the Federation for a short time after the death of Lord Llewellin in 1957 (he followed Sir Robert Tredgold who was also acting Governor General for a short time).

14 **poll-tax**
A tax of a fixed amount which is levied on every person of a specified class, especially as a prerequisite to the right to vote in elections. In Rhodesia, from 1953, the "qualified franchise" gave the vote to nearly all adult Europeans but denied that same right to vote to most Africans.

16 **'Baas'**
'Boss' or 'Master'.

19 **Cicadas**
Tropical insects which live on trees and shrubs. The male makes a shrill whistling sound.

20 **kudu**
Large African antelopes. Their greyish-brown coats have vertical white stripes on the flanks and the male has spirally twisted horns. The species is protected.

23 **kopje**
Afrikaans *koppie*, a diminutive of *kop*, a hillock on the veld, covered with scrub.

30 **vleis and veld**
Vleis is Afrikaans for 'valley' and denotes a shallow, marshy depression in an arid expanse of veld, in which water collects in the rainy season.
The veld is the unenclosed plains of southern Africa. There are scattered shrubs and bushes on the veld but very few trees.

31 **sjambok's thong**
Sjambok is Afrikaans for a strong and heavy whip, usually made of rhinoceros or hippopotamus hide. It is used in southern Africa for driving cattle and sometimes for whipping.

35 **mealie**
Afrikaans *milje*, maize or Indian corn, a staple in Africa.
tsetse flies
Bloodsucking insects that occur in Africa south of the Sahara. Their bite is fatal to domestic animals, and they act as a vector of sleeping sickness in man.

37 **red-hot poker**

Also called torch lily. A robust perennial which grows in clusters on the open veld. The reddish buds change to yellow when the flower opens.

V 4 **sunbird**
A small perching bird of the passerine family. They are principally flower birds, flitting about and perching on blossoms, looking for insects and nectar with their long bills.

6 **the weaver's nest**
The weaver, a small tropical bird resembling a finch, is so named because of its elaborately woven nest—a roofed, hanging chamber.

7 **a high dam**
The Kariba dam on the Zambesi between Southern and Northern Rhodesia (now Zambia), built for a hydroelectric project to serve the copper-belt towns. The generating station is on what was Southern Rhodesian territory. The dam was built between 1955 and 1959, at a cost of more than £100 million, and the hydroelectric scheme was officially opened on 17 May 1960.

8 **Where once the Zambesi was worshipped**
The land to be flooded to create the artificial lake was sparsely populated, but about 50,000 river-dwellers of the Tonga tribe had to be resettled.

12 **The leopards he shipped to the Dublin zoo**
Sent from Ceylon during the nineteen thirties.

VI 6 **rinderpest**
German *rinder* (cattle) and *pest* (plague). A virulent, infectious disease, endemic in central and southern Africa, which affects all ruminant animals, especially oxen. It is characterised by fever and dysentery.

9 **mopani**
A narrow-crowned tree of the pea family found in tropical Africa. Its wood is used for lumber, fencing-posts and pit-props.

10 **laagers**
Afrikaans for an encampment, usually defensive and marked out by a circle of wagons or armoured vehicles. The word describes people drawn together in a definite

group because of their ideals, e.g., the *verkrampte laager*.

12 **assegais**
Arabic word for the slender hardwood spears or javelins, usually tipped with iron, that were once the chief weapon of the Zulus and some other African tribes.

14 **Sundowners**
The name, in colonial societies, for the first drink of the evening.

15 **the Munts**
A colloquial equivalent of the Zulu *umunthu* (person), which is used derogatively of the African male by certain whites

17 **Ithaca**
A small island in the Ionian Sea, off the west coast of Greece, which was reputedly the home of Odysseus. See the reference to Homer, IV, 10. Cf. Cavafy's poem "Ithaca".

18 **BSA police**
The British South Africa Police.

19 *Pax Britannica*
The peace formerly imposed by Britain in her colonial empire. The phrase is modelled on *Pax Romana*, the peace existing between the various parts of the Roman empire.

21 **stoep**
Afrikaans for a covered verandah running along the front and sometimes around the sides of a house of Dutch architecture. 'Stoop' is the American equivalent.

Mary FitzGerald

A Richard Murphy Bibliography

PUBLISHED WORKS OF RICHARD MURPHY

Volumes of Poetry and Recordings

The Archaeology of Love: Poems. Glenageary: Dolmen, 1955.
Sailing to an Island: A Poem. Dublin: privately printed at the Dolmen Press, 1955. 35 numbered copies.
The Woman of the House: An Elegy. Dublin: Dolmen, 1959.
The Last Galway Hooker. Dublin: Dolmen, 1961.
Sailing to an Island. London: Faber and Faber, 1963; New York: Chilmark Press, 1964.
The Battle of Aughrim and *The God Who Eats Corn.* London: Faber and Faber; New York: Alfred A. Knopf, 1968.
The Battle of Aughrim. London: Claddagh Records, 1969.
High Island. London: Faber and Faber, 1974.
High Island. New and Selected Poems. New York and London: Harper and Row, 1974. [Includes sections of *Sailing to an Island*, as well as the full texts of *The Battle of Aughrim* and *The God Who Eats Corn*, and *High Island*.]

Poems Published in Periodicals

"Aasleagh in Autumn". *The Irish Times*, 17 January 1953, p. 6.
"Advice about Wind". *The Bell*, 18 (March 1953), pp. 586-88.
"Afternoon at Home". *The Listener*, 9 April 1953, p. 594.
"An Air Raid Siren in Peacetime". *The Irish Times*, 4 February 1956, p. 6.
"Around the World in Ninety Hours". *The Listener*, 16 January 1958, p. 132.
"Auction". *Encounter*, 5 (August 1955), p. 50.
"Ball's Cove". *Hibernia*, 37 (30 March 1973), p. 14; *The London Magazine*, New Series, 13 (April/May 1973), p. 20.
"The Battle of Aughrim". *New Statesman*, 6 September 1953, p. 289.
"Brian Boru's Well". *The London Magazine*, New Series, 13

(April/May 1973), p. 19.

"Christening". *Hibernia*, 31 (February 1967), p. 22.

"Circumcision at the Temple". *The Listener*, 16 September 1954, p. 437.

"The Cleggan Disaster". *Prose and Verse Readings: BBC Broadcasts to Schools*, Spring 1963, pp. 24-33.

"The Clown and the Garden". *The Irish Times*, 26 March 1955, p. 6.

"Coppersmith". *The London Magazine*, New Series, 14 (October/November 1974), p. 48.

"Corncrake". *Poetry*, 118 (September 1971), pp. 334-35.

"Cove of Trees". *The Listener*, 19 March 1953, p. 480.

"Creragh". *The Bell*, 16 (December 1950), p. 16.

"Double Negative". *The New Review*, 1 (September 1974), p. 47.

"The Dozing Woods". *The Irish Times*, 20 June 1953, p. 6.

"Eclogue in the Louvre". *The Listener*, 6 January 1955, p. 16.

"Elegy for a Battle". *Massachusetts Review*, 5 (Winter 1964), pp. 250-55.

"Emigration". *The Irish Times*, 3 February 1951, p. 6.

"Epitaph on a Fir Tree". *The Irish Times*, 9 June 1956, p. 6.; *Listen*, 2 (Spring 1959), p. 7.

"The Exiled Fisherman". *The Irish Times*, 24 April 1954, p. 8.

"A Fable for Lovers". *Listen*, 2 (Spring 1959), pp. 6-7.

"The Fall". *The London Magazine*, New Series, 14 (October/November 1974), pp. 49-50.

"Fall of Knossus". *New Statesman*, 18 December 1954, p. 832.

"Firebug". *The New York Review of Books*, 16 November 1972, p. 6; *The London Magazine*, New Series, 14 (October/November 1974), p. 47.

"Gallows Riddle". *Poetry*, 118 (September 1971), p. 335.

"Girl at Seaside". *Encounter*, 5 (August 1955), p. 50.

"The Glass Dump Road". *The New York Review of Books*, 29 November 1973, p. 25; *Austin Clarke Memorial Broadsheet*, [October 1975].

"The God Who Eats Corn". *The Reporter*, 7 May 1964, pp. 34-36; *The Listener*, 6 August 1964, pp. 191-92.

"Granite Globe". *The New Review*, 1 (September 1974), p. 47.

"Graves at Inishbofin". *The Irish Times*, 28 January 1961, p. 14.

"The Halcyon Days: Crete". *The Listener*, 7 January 1954, p. 14.

"High Island". *The American Review*, 21 (October 1974), pp. 144-45.

"Houses". *The Irish Times*, 9 July 1955, p. 6.

"The Island Girl". *Listen*, 3 (Spring 1960), pp. 3-4.

"Jurors". *The New Review*, 1 (September 1974), p. 46.
"The Lake at Carrahall". *The Irish Times*, 19 November 1955, p. 6.
"The Last Galway Hooker". *The Listener*, 9 February 1961, p. 274.
"Latch". *Listen*, 4 (Autumn 1962), p. 7; *The Dubliner*, 6 (January/February 1963), p. 52.
"Letter from Babylone". *The Listener*, 23 December 1955, p. 1113.
"Letter to a Friend Leaving Ireland". *The Irish Times*, 22 May 1954, p. 6.
"Little Hunger". *Poetry*, 118 (September 1971), p. 334; *The Irish Press*, 22 April 1972.
"Living with Animals". *The Listener*, 20 October 1955, p. 653.
"Lullaby". *The New Review*, 1 (September 1974), p. 46.
"Mary Ure". *The Times Literary Supplement*, 18 July 1975, p. 790.
"Miscarriage". *Listen*, 2 (Spring 1959), p. 6.
"My Three and Twentieth Year". *Envoy*, 13 December 1950, p. 49.
"The Netting". *The Yale Review*, 50 (June 1969), pp. 567-68.
"Overboard". *The London Magazine*, New Series, 13 (April/May 1973), p. 22.
"Pat Cloherty's Version of *The Maisie*". *Stand*, 15 (1974), pp. 8-9.
"Payday". *The Irish Times*, 11 April 1953, p. 6.
"The Philosopher and the Birds". *Adelphi*, 29 (April 1953), pp. 342-43.
"The Poet on the Island". *Poetry*, 98 (July 1961), pp. 224-25; *The Dubliner*, 6 (January/February 1963), pp. 51-52.
"The Progress of a Painter". *Poetry at the Mermaid: Souvenir Programme*, 1961, pp. 51-52.
"The Reading Lesson". *The New York Review of Books*, 21 October 1971, p. 11; *The Irish Press*, 22 April 1972.
"The Restoration". *The Irish Times*, 13 December 1952, p. 6.
"The Return". *The Bell*, 18 (March 1953), pp. 583-86.
"Saint Gormgall's Well". *Poetry*, 118 (September 1971), pp. 333-34; *The Irish Press*, 22 April 1972.
"Samson's Secret". *Encounter*, 5 (August 1955), p. 50.
"Seals at High Island". *The New York Review of Books*, 22 February 1973, p. 24; *The London Magazine*, New Series, 13 (April/May 1973), pp. 21-22; *Austin Clarke Memorial Broadsheet*, [October 1975].
"September on the Embankment". *The Listener*, 7 October 1954,

p. 558.

"Shelter". *The Sewanee Review*, 84 (Winter 1976), pp. 127-28; *Austin Clarke Broadsheet*, 2.

"The Singing Wood". *The Irish Times*, 10 July 1954, p. 8.

"The Sisters". *The Irish Times*, 16 October 1954, p. 6.

"Slate". *St Stephen's*, Trinity Term 1966, p. 8.

"Snow". *The Listener*, 27 September 1951, p. 499.

"Song for a Corncrake". *The Times Literary Supplement*, 3 March 1972, p. 314.

"Stormpetrel". *The New Review*, 1 September 1974, p. 48.

"Sun and Thorn". *The Irish Times*, 5 September 1953, p. 6.

"Swallows". *The Sewanee Review*, 84 (Winter 1976), p. 128; *Austin Clarke Broadsheet*, 2.

"To a Cretan Monk in Thanks for a Flask of Wine". *The Irish Times*, 22 October 1955, p. 6.

"Traveller's Palm". *The New York Review of Books*, 31 October 1974, p. 34; *The London Magazine*, 14 (October/November 1974), pp. 50-52.

"Travelling Man". *The New Review*, 6 (September 1974), p. 48.

"The Travelling Player". *The Irish Times*, 8 December 1962, p. 6.

"Trouvaille". *The Times Literary Supplement*, 25 July 1975, p. 838.

"Voyage to an Island". *The Bell*, 18 (December 1952), pp. 396-400; *Listen*, 1 (Winter 1954), pp. 39-40.

"A West Indian Village". *The Irish Times*, 21 June 1952, p. 6.

"Wild Geese". *The Irish Times*, 23 May 1959, p. 6.

"The Woman of the House". *The Listener*, 23 April 1959, p. 723.

"The Writing Lesson". *The London Magazine*, New Series 14 (October/November 1974), pp. 47-48.

"Years Later; The Epilogue to *The Cleggan Disaster*". *Handbook of the Cheltenham Festival of Literature*. Cheltenham: Festival Arts, Ltd., 1962.

Anthologies

Beer, Patricia (ed.) *New Poems 1975*. London: Hutchinson, 1975.

Beer, Patricia, Ted Hughes, and Vernon Scannell (eds.) *New Poems 1962*. London: Hutchinson, 1962.

Betjeman, John and Geoffrey Taylor (eds.) *English Love Poems*. London: Faber and Faber, 1957.

Carroll, Donald (ed.) *New Poets of Ireland*. Denver, Colorado: Alan Swallow, 1963.

Cole, William (ed.) *Poems from Ireland*. New York: Thomas Y.

Crowell, 1972.

Dunn, Douglas (ed.) *New Poems 1972-73*. London: Hutchinson, 1973.

Dyment, Clifford, Roy Fuller and Montague Slater (eds.) *New Poems 1952*. London: Michael Joseph, 1952.

Fauchereau, Serge (ed.) "Ecrivains irlandais d'aujourd'hui", *Les Lettres Nouvelles*, Numéro spécial, mars 1973. [English with French translation.]

Fraser, G.S. (ed.) *Poetry Now*. London: Faber and Faber, 1956.

The Guinness Book of Poetry 1958-59. London: Putnam, 1960.

Heaney, Seamus (ed.) *Soundings '72: An annual anthology of new Irish.Poetry*. Belfast: Blackstaff Press, 1972.

Heaney, Seamus (ed.) *Soundings 2: An annual anthology of new Irish Poetry*. Belfast: Blackstaff Press, 1974.

Heath-Stubbs, John and David Wright (eds.) *The Faber Book of Twentieth Century Verse*, revised edition. London: Faber and Faber, 1965.

Kennelly, Brendan (ed.) *The Penguin Book of Irish Verse*. Harmondsworth, Baltimore and Ringwood: Penguin Books, 1970.

Lask, Thomas (ed.) *The New York Times Book of Verse*. New York: Macmillan, 1962.

Lucy, Seán (ed.) *Love Poems of the Irish*. Cork: Mercier Press, 1967.

Mahon, Derek (ed.) *The Sphere Book of Modern Irish Poetry*. London: Sphere Books, 1972.

Marcus, David (ed.) *Irish Poets 1924-1974*. London: Pan Books, 1975.

Moat, John (ed.) *A Standard of Verse and nine poems*. Newbury, Berkshire: Phoenix Press, 1969.

Montague, John (ed.) *An Anthology of Irish Poetry From the Sixth Century to the Present*. New York: Macmillan, 1977.

Montague, John (ed.) *The Dolmen Anthology of Irish Writing*. Dublin: Dolmen Press; New York and London: Oxford University Press, 1962.

Montague, John (ed.) *The Faber Book of Irish Verse*. London: Faber and Faber, 1976.

Penguin Modern Poets 7. London: Penguin, 1965. [With Jon Silkin and Nathaniel Tarn.]

Quinn, Bridie and Seamus Cashman (eds.) *The Wolfhound Book of Irish Poems for Young People*. [Dublin] : The Wolfhound Press, 1975.

Rosenthal, M.L. (ed.) *The New Modern Poetry: British and*

American Poetry since World War II. New York: Macmillan, 1967.

Rosenthal, M.L. (ed.) *100 Postwar Poems: British and American*. New York: Macmillan, 1968.

Skelton, Robin (ed.) *Six Irish Poets*. London and New York: Oxford University Press, 1962.

Three Irish Poets: John Montague, Thomas Kinsella, Richard Murphy. Dublin: Dolmen Press, 1961.

Criticism and Reviews

"American Poetry". *The Spectator*, 2 February 1951, p. 152. Review: *The Oxford Book of American Verse*, ed. F.O. Matthiessen.

"Appreciation of Milton". *The Times Literary Supplement*, 15 May 1953, p. 318. Review: *Milton's Act of Prosody*, S. Ernest Sprott.

"The Art of a Translator". *The Spectator*, 18 September 1953. pp. 303-04. Review: *The Translations of Ezra Pound*, ed. D.D. Paige.

"The Art of Debunkery". *The New York Review of Books*, 15 May 1975, pp. 30-33. Review: *High Windows*, Philip Larkin.

"Before Yeats". *The Times Educational Supplement*, 13 April 1951, p. 279. Review: *Irish Poets of the Nineteenth Century*, ed. Geoffrey Taylor.

"Charm of Eire". *The Listener*, 16 January 1958, p. 119.

"The Clumsy Blue Bird". *The Spectator*, 26 June 1953, p. 838. Review: *Selected Poems*, Idris Davies; *Famous Meeting*, Robert Gittings; *A Mask for Janus*, W.S. Merwin.

"The Critic and Society". *The Spectator*, 8 May 1953, p. 582. Review: *The Responsibilities of the Critic*, F.O. Matthiessen.

"Donne and Milton". *The Spectator*, 20 March 1953, pp. 352-54. Review: *John Donne: The Divine Poems*, ed. Helen Gardner; *The Poetical Works of John Milton*, Vol. I, ed. Helen Darbishire.

"Drayton's Discovery of England". *The Times Literary Supplement*, 8 May 1953, p. 303. Review: *Poems of Michael Drayton*, ed. John Buxton.

"Essay in Verse". *The Times Literary Supplement*, 26 June 1953, p. 416. Review: *Letter in a Bottle*, Gerald B. Walker.

"Irish Poetry Today". *The Dubliner*, 6 (January/December 1963), pp. 64-81. Review: *Six Irish Poets*, ed. Robin Skelton.

"The Irish Situation". *The New York Review of Books*, 17 April 1975, p. 38. Letter replying to Donald Davie's review of *High*

Island of 12 April.

"Landsman Hay". *The Listener*, 26 November 1953, p. 917. Review: *Memoirs of Robert Hay, 1789-1847*, ed. M.D. Hay.

"The Mind of Coleridge". *The Spectator*, 31 July 1953, pp. 133-34. Review: *Coleridge: The Clark Lectures, 1951-52*, Humphry House.

"The Muse in Chains". *The Times Literary Supplement*, 17 June 1960, p. 385. Letter in metrics controversy over *The Woman of the House*. [See following entries under this title, p. 114.]

"The Music of Poetry". *The Spectator*, 13 February 1953. pp. 191-92. Review: *Selected Poems*, Wallace Stevens.

"New Beauty for Old Clay". *The New York Times Book Review*, 23 March 1965, p. 4. Review: *Collected Poems*, Patrick Kavanagh.

"The Pleasure Ground". *Writers on Themselves*. London: British Broadcasting Corporation, 1964, pp. 62-66; *The Listener*, 15 August 1963, p. 226.

"Poetry and Terror". *The New York Review of Books*, 30 September 1976, pp. 38-40. Review: *North*, Seamus Heaney.

"Random Pleasure". *The Spectator*, 13 November 1953, pp. 543-44. Review: *The Faber Book of Twentieth Century Verse*, ed. John Heath-Stubbs and David Wright.

"The Sea! The Sea!" *The Spectator*, 2 October 1953, pp. 372-73. Review: *Journey into Wonder*, N.J. Berrill, *The Ocean River*, Henry Chapin and F.G. Walton Smith, and *The Voyage of Waltzing Matilda*, Philip Davenport.

"Somewhat like Poetry". *The Spectator*, 10 July 1953, pp. 68-70. Review: *The Singing Reel*, Moray McLaren.

"A Storyteller in Verse". *The Spectator*, 4 May 1951, p. 594. Review: *Collected Poems*, Robert Frost.

"A Study of Shakespeare". *The Spectator*, 15 May, 1953, pp. 648-50. Review: *Shakespeare*, Henri Fluchère.

"Studying Poetry". *The Times Literary Supplement*, 31 July 1953, p. 494. Review: *The Anatomy of Poetry*, Marjorie Boulton.

"To Celebrate Existence". *Hibernia*, 17 December 1976. Review: *Season Songs*, Ted Hughes.

"Three Modern . Poets". *The Listener*, 9 September 1955, pp. 373-75. Criticism. [Theodore Roethke, Philip Larkin, Valentin Iremonger].

"Wholesome". *The Spectator*, 11 September 1953, p. 278. Review: *J.P. Marquand, Esquire*, Philip Hamburger.

"Why Has Narrative Poetry Failed?" *The Listener*, 9 August 1951, pp. 226-27. Criticism.

CRITICISM AND REVIEWS OF PUBLISHED WORK OF RICHARD MURPHY

Articles Wholly or Partly about Richard Murphy

Boland, John. "Bouquets for Cacoyannis/Superb playing at Abbey". *The Irish Press*, 5 April 1973, p. 3. Review of *King Oedipus* with comments on RM's additions to the text.

Boland, John. "Relating to our past". *The Irish Press*, 7 June 1973, p. 17. Interview with RM.

The Bookseller, 2 March 1963, p. 42. Announcement that *Sailing to an Island* is choice of The Poetry Book Society.

Brownlow, Timothy. "Poet and Gentleman". *Hibernia*, 31 (February 1967), p. 22.

Carew, Rivers. "Review of 1968 Poetry". *Hibernia*, 33 (January 1969), p. 14.

Colgate Maroon, 23 February 1971, p. 5. Description of poetry reading.

"Commentary". *The Times Literary Supplement*, 29 May 1970, p. 423. Refers to United States tour by Ted Hughes and RM.

"Connemara Fishing Trips Popular". *Irish Independent*, 17 January 1962, p. 8. RM's Galway hooker.

Cunningham, John. "A poet on campus". *The Guardian*, 31 May 1969, p. 7. RM as writer in residence at the University of Hull.

Fiacc, Padraic. "Isolation in Contemporary Ireland: the AE Winners". *Hibernia*, December 1975, p. 23.

Gillespie, Elgy. "Richard Murphy upon Omey". *The Irish Times*, 21 November 1975, p. 10. Interview with RM.

Gillespie, Elgy. "Robert Lowell in Kilkenny". *The Irish Times*, 4 September 1975, p. 8. Mentions RM at Kilkenny Arts Festival.

Harmon, Maurice. "New Voices in the Fifties". *Irish Poets in English*, ed. Sean Lucy. Cork and Dublin: Mercier Press, 1973. pp. 185-207.

Harmon, Maurice. "By Memory Inspired: Themes and Forces in Recent Irish Writing". *Eire-Ireland*, 8 (Summer 1973), pp. 3-19.

"He Handed Over the Last of the Galway Hookers". *Sunday Press*, 1 October 1961, p. 5. RM mentioned as buyer.

Healy, Isabel. "In Cleggan, Co Galway, Isabel Healy met . . ./ Richard Murphy: a poet in a pink granite house". *The Irish Press*, 3 November 1971, p. 5. Interview with RM.

Irish Independent, 24 December 1962, p. 6. Announcement of reading of *Sailing to an Island* on Rádio Telefis Eireann.

Irish Press, The, 22 December 1962, p. 4. Announcement of reading of "The Cleggan Disaster" on Radio Telefis Eireann.

"Irish Writer's Poem on B.B.C.". *The Irish Times*, 4 August 1962, p. 9. Announcement of reading of *The God Who Eats Corn.*

"Irishman Wins Guinness Prize for Poetry". *The Irish Times*, 4 August 1962, p. 9.

Kay, Ernest, ed. *International Who's Who in Poetry*, 4th ed. Cambridge and London: Melrose Press, 1974, pp. 326-27.

Kennelly, Brendan. "Introduction". *The Penguin Book of Irish Verse*, ed. Brendan Kennelly. Harmondsworth, Baltimore and Ringwood: Penguin Books, 1970, pp. 29-42.

Kersnowski, Frank. *The Outsiders: Poets of Contemporary Ireland*. Fort Worth, Texas: Texas Christian University Press, 1975, pp. 93-98, 160-61, 171.

Kersnowski, Frank, C.W. Spinks, and Laird Loomis. *A Bibliography of Modern Irish and Anglo-Irish Literature*. San Antonio, Texas: Trinity University Press, 1976, p. 86.

Kinsella, Thomas. "Richard Murphy", in *Contemporary Poets of The English Language*. ed. Rosalie Murphy, James Vinson. Chicago and London: St James Press, 1970, pp. 784-85; 2nd ed. by James Vinson and D.L. Kirkpatrick. London: St James Press; New York: St Martin's Press, 1975, pp. 1094-95.

Kramer, A. Walter. "The African Connection". *The Reporter*, 4 June 1968, p. 6.

"Last of Claddagh Hookers Has Moved to Cleggan". *Connaught Tribune*, 7 October 1961, p. 4. Mentions RM as buyer.

Lewsen, Charles. "Cacoyannis Shows Little Daring/Oedipus/Abbey, Dublin". *The Times* [London], 6 April 1973, p. 15. Comments on RM's additions to the text.

"London Letter". *The Irish Times*, 22 February 1963, p. 7. Mentions embassy reception for RM.

Longley, Edna. "Searching the Darkness: Richard Murphy, Thomas Kinsella, John Montague and James Simmons", in *Two Decades of Irish Writing: A Critical Survey*. ed. Douglas Dunn. Cheadle Hulme: Carcanet Press, 1975, pp. 118-53.

MacConnell, Cormac. "A Poet on his own Island: Annalist of the Galway Hooker". *The Irish Press*, 22 January 1976, p. 9.

MacIntyre, Tom. "The Storied Stones of Inishbofin". *Cara: the inflight magazine of Aer Lingus*, 7 (October/November 1974), pp. 26-27. Unidentified quotation from "The Battle of Aughrim".

MacMahon, Bryan. "Place and People into Poetry", in *Irish Poets in English*. ed. Sean Lucy. Cork and Dublin: Mercier Press, 1973, pp. 60-74.

Mahon, Derek. Introduction to *The Sphere Book of Modern Irish Poetry*, ed. Derek Mahon. London: Sphere Books, 1972, pp. 11-15.

Manning, Mary. "More Visiting Directors Please". *Hibernia*, 37 (13 April 1973), p. 27. Mentions RM's additions to the text of Yeats's *King Oedipus*.

Montague, John. "In the Irish Grain". *The Faber Book of Irish Verse*. ed. John Montague. London: Faber and Faber, 1974; *An Anthology of Irish Poetry From the Sixth Century to the Present*. ed. John Montague. New York: Macmillan, 1977; pp. 21-39.

Montague, John. "Order in Donnybrook Fair". *The Times Literary Supplement*, 17 March 1972, p. 313.

"Poet of High Island". *RTE Guide*, 9 January 1976, p. 11. Mentions RM's radio appearances.

"Poet spends prize to aid itinerants". *The Irish Times*, 15 December 1967, p. 8.

Quidnunc, "An Irishman's Diary". *The Irish Times*, 3 February 1965, p. 7. Mentions RM's reading at University College, Dublin.

Quidnunc. "An Irishman's Diary". *The Irish Times*, 4 April 1973, p. 11. Quotes RM and comments about additions to the text of Yeats's *King Oedipus*.

Rushe, Desmond. "Abbey's 'Oedipus' Immensely Live". *Irish Independent*, 5 April 1973, p. 28.

Rushe, Desmond. "Tatler's Parade". *Irish Independent*, 10 April 1973, p. 10. Mentions RM's additions to text of Yeats's *King Oedipus*.

"Russell Memorial Prize Winner". *The Irish Times*, 5 April 1951, p. 5.

Schull, Rebecca. "The Preparation of King Oedipus". *The Arts in Ireland*, 2 (1973), pp. 15-21. Quotes RM; mentions additions to text of play.

Schull, Rebecca. "Rebecca Schull talks to the poet Richard Murphy about his recently completed additions to the W.B. Yeats version of Sophocles' 'King Oedipus' for the Abbey Theatre, and about his own background". *The Irish Times*, 17 May 1973, p. 12. Consists entirely of quotations from RM.

"U.S. college chair for poet Murphy". *Irish Independent*, 6 January 1971, p. 9. Announces RM's appointment to Colgate and proposed tour of the United States with Ted Hughes.

Wright, Fergus. "Lots of Luck for Literary Men". *Sunday Independent*, 23 December 1962, p. 13. Announces RM broadcast.

Reviews

Reviews: The Woman of the House: An Elegy
Corke, Hilary. "Is Metre a Dirty Word?: and other observations on the present state of poetry". *The London Magazine*, 7 (April 1960), pp. 52-62. Negative view of modern metrics, which prompted an exchange of letters entitled "The Muse in Chains" [given here in chronological order of their appearance].

"Commentary". *The Times Literary Supplement*, 13 May 1960, p. 305.

Corke, Hilary. Letter. *The Times Literary Supplement*, 27 May 1960, p. 339.

Fraser, G.S. Letter. *The Times Literary Supplement*, 3 June 1960, p. 353.

Corke, Hilary. Letter. *The Times Literary Supplement*, 17 June 1960. p. 385.

Murphy, Richard. Letter. *The Times Literary Supplement*, 17 June 1960, p. 385.

Fraser, G.S. Letter. *The Times Literary Supplement*, 24 June 1960, p. 401.

Hawkes, Terence. Letter. *The Times Literary Supplement*, 1 July 1960, p. 417.

Corke, Hilary. Letter. *The Times Literary Supplement*, 8 July 1960, p. 433.

Fraser, G.S. Letter. *The Times Literary Supplement*, 8 July 1960, p. 433.

Fenwick, J.H. Letter. *The London Magazine*, 1 (July 1960), pp. 69-70.

Hawkes, Terence. Letter. *The Times Literary Supplement*, 15 July 1960, p. 456.

Corke, Hilary. Letter. *The Times Literary Supplement*, 29 July 1960, p. 481.

Empson, William. Letter. *The Times Literary Supplement*, 5 August 1960, p. 497.

Hawkes, Terence. Letter. *The Times Literary Supplement*, 5 August 1960, p. 497.

Hewitt, John. *Threshold*, 3 (Summer 1959), pp. 92-96.

Reviews: The Last Galway Hooker

Davie, Donald. *New Statesman*, 21 July 1961, pp. 91-92.

H[ewitt], J[ohn]. *Threshold*, 5 (Autumn-Winter 1961-62), pp. 75-81.

Holzapfel, Rudi. *The Kilkenny Magazine*, 5 (Autumn-Winter 1961), p. 59.

Reviews: Sailing to an Island

Fadiman, Clifton. Dustjacket of *Sailing to an Island*. New York: Chilmark Press, 1964.

Fairfax, John. *Poetry Review* [London], 52 (Summer 1963), p. 191.

Fandel, John. *Commonweal*, 8 May 1964, p. 212.

Furbank, P.N. *The Listener*, 7 March 1963, p. 435.

H., T. *The Kilkenny Magazine*, 9 (Spring 1963), pp. 74-75.

Harkness, Marjory Gane. *The Laconia Evening Citizen*, 25 November 1964, p. 1.

H[ealy], I[sabel]. *Irish Independent*, 12/13 April 1963, p. 12.

Heaney, Seamus. *Hibernia*, 27 (July 1963), p. 17.

Kell, Richard. *The Guardian*, 22 March 1963, p. 9.

Lask, Thomas. *The New York Times Book Review*, 25 October 1963, p. 29.

M., J. *Yachting Monthly*, 114 (April 1963), p. 208.

MacBeth, George. *London Mercury*, (July 1963), p. 87.

MacCaig, Norman. *New Statesman*, 15 March 1963, p. 387.

Makin, John. Trinidad Radio, n.d.

Martin, Augustine. *Studies*, 53 (Spring 1964), pp. 95-99.

Martin, Graham. *The Review*, 8 (August 1963), pp. 18-20.

Mercedes, Sr. Anna. *Spirit*, 31 (September 1964), p. 112.

Reynolds, Lorna. *University Review*, 3 (1963), pp. 60-61.

Rosenthal, M.L. *The New York Times Book Review*, 22 December 1963, pp. 4-5.

S., (D.H.), *The Dubliner*, 2 (Summer 1963), pp. 88-90.

Sandford, Antonia. *Books and Bookmen*, 8 (April 1963), p. 30.

Stallworthy, Jon. *Critical Quarterly*, 5 (Summer 1963), p. 187.

Symons, Julian. *The Spectator*, 10 May 1963, p. 606.

Thomas, Gilbert. *The Birmingham Post*, 19 March 1963, p. 22.

Walsh, Chad. *Book Week*, 29 December 1963, p. 8.

Reviews: Penguin Modern Poets 7

Cox, C.B., *The Spectator*, 1 April 1966, p. 411.

Levi, Peter. *The Tablet* [London], 19 February 1966, p. 216.

Kelly, Hugh. *The Dublin Magazine*, 5 (Autumn-Winter 1966), p. 110.

Reviews: The Battle of Aughrim *and* The God Who Eats Corn

Andrews, Lyman. *The Sunday Times*, 19 January 1969, p. 32.

Boland, Eavan. *The Irish Times*, 1 March 1969, p. 8.

Brownjohn, Alan. *New Statesman*, 20 September 1968, pp. 362-63.

Colum, Padraic. *The New York Times Book Review*, 2 March 1969, pp. 10-12.

Delehanty, James. *The Kilkenny Magazine*, 16-17 (Spring 1969), pp. 153-57.

Dodsworth, Martin. *The Listener*, 27 March 1969, p. 434.

Ewart, Gavin. *The London Magazine*, 8 (December 1968), p. 92.

Fauchereau, Serge. *Critique* [Paris], 26 (May 1970), pp. 438-56.

Hamilton, Ian. *The Observer*, 17 November 1968, p. 28.

Hanshell, Deryck, S.J., *The Tablet*, 21 September 1968, p. 939.

Hoffman, Daniel. *Poetry*, 114 (August 1969), pp. 342-44.

Holmes, Richard. *The Times Saturday Review*, 19 April 1969, p. 22.

Jordan, John. *Hibernia*, 32 (13 December 1968), p. 18.

Kavanagh, P.J. *The Guardian*, 11 October 1968, p. 9.

Kell, Richard. *The Critical Survey*, 4 (Summer 1969), pp. 125-28.

Kirkus Reviews, 15 July 1968, p. 803.

MacInerney, John. *St Stephen's*, Michaelmas Term 1968, pp. 29-34.

Martin, Augustine. *The Irish Press*, 5 October 1968, p. 10.

Payne, Basil. *Studies*, 58 (Spring 1969), pp. 74-78.

Reynolds, Gillian. *The Guardian*, 21 September 1968, p. 7.

Sergeant, Howard. *English*, 18 (Spring 1969), pp. 33-36.

Thwaite, Anthony. *New Statesman*, 21 February 1970, pp. 268-69.

Times Literary Supplement, The, 5 December 1968, p. 1386.

Wall, Stephen. *The Review*, 20 (March 1969), pp. 57-60.

Walsh, Chad. *Book World*, 3 November 1968, p. 20.

Waring, Walter. *Library Journal*, 15 September 1968, p. 3145.

Yeats, Michael. *Evening Press*, 27 December 1969, p. 6.

Reviews: High Island

American Libraries, November 1974, p. 548.

Andrews, Lyman. *The Sunday Times*, 9 March 1975, p. 28.

Boland, John. *Hibernia*, 39 (10 January 1975), p. 29.

Booklist, 15 January 1975, p. 480.

Brownjohn, Alan. *New Statesman*, 14 March 1975, p. 346-47.

Brownlow, Timothy. *Oxford Literary Review*, (Winter 1974), pp. 17-18.

Choice, 12 (May 1975), p. 393.

Davie, Donald. *The New York Review of Books*, 6 March 1975, pp. 10-11.

Davie, Donald. Letter. *The New York Review of Books*, 17 April 1975, p. 38.

Deane, Seamus. *The Sewanee Review*, 84 (Winter 1976), pp. 199-201.

Dunn, Douglas. *Encounter*, 44 (May 1975), pp. 73-76.

Eagleton, Terry. *The Tablet*, 15 February 1975, pp. 154-55.

Falck, Colin. *The New Review*. 1 (February 1975), pp. 69-71.

Harmon, Maurice. *Irish University Review*, 5 (Spring 1975), pp. 201-02.

Heaney, Seamus. *Imprint*, Radio Telefis Eireann, 27 January 1975.

Hibernia, 31 (April 1967), p. 16.

Howe, Parkman. *The Christian Science Monitor*, 22 October 1975, p. 18.

Irish Echo, 22 February 1975, p. 3.

Kirkus Reviews, 15 September 1974, p. 1046.

Montague, John. *The Times Literary Supplement*, 4 July 1975, p. 718.

Sealy, Douglas. *The Irish Press*, 25 January 1975, p. 6.

Stevenson, Anne. *The Listener*, 30 October 1975, p. 571.

Willingham, J.R. *Library Journal*, 15 December 1974, p. 3203.

Young, Vernon. *The Hudson Review*, 83 (Winter 1975), pp. 585-600.

Maurice Harmon

Beginning With Words

In an early rooting of the self, Richard Murphy defined himself as a follower of Wittgenstein, who "broke prisons, beginning with words." When he left Oxford in 1951 and went to live in the west of Ireland, he found himself in a house previously inhabited by the philosopher. The poem, "The Philosopher and the Birds," defines the succession in specific terms: Wittgenstein had also exchanged university for Connemara, had a similar sense of temporal perspectives, and shared a responsiveness to the natural setting. Wittgenstein's relationship to the landscape of the west and to the creatures of that landscape has two sides to it. On one side is the portrait of the self as rational observer, entering into a controlled and controlling relationship with the birds: he "tamed, by talking, wild birds." On the other side is the portrait of the self as irrational victim, unable to master external reality: "haunted by gulls . . . /His nerve tormented by terrified knots/ In pin-feathered flesh." Wittgenstein knew that the problems of thought are problems of language, but went beyond words to the area of untameable wildness. When Murphy defines his own act of faith in this master, he carefully takes on the duality of growth and death:

.... now by belief
I follow his love which bird-handled thoughts
To grasp growth's terror or death's leaf.

"The Philosopher and the Birds" turns upon intuitions of the processes of growth and change that go beyond any single interpretation, but in the light of Murphy's development as a poet and of the directions and emphases of his work, it is useful to note the tension in this poem between the two sides of the self. Normally, we think of the persona in a Murphy poem as rational and civilised, a sensibility with a feeling for language and with an appreciation of materials—stone, wood, words. At the same time there are a number of places in his work where the persona suffers from a failure to relate to experience with the necessary skills.

The emphasis on words appears elsewhere in *The Archaeology*

118

of Love (1955). The poet's characteristic awareness of ancestry and his feelings for materials are present in "Houses" and "Auction". He states his own position quietly:

> With what shall I buy
> From time's auctioneers
> This property?
> Poor word's I'll offer.

In "Letter from Babylone", he writes, "So I send you these words": the poem is descriptive of a place to which the "you" figure will also come. More than once we hear the note of the pain involved in the making of poetry. The poems with settings in Crete and Greece celebrate the growth of love and its transforming effect of outlook, which includes the hazardous freeing of language. "I swear I will upset death's duty/And be the victim for words to dine."

Intimations of grief and destruction recur in the *Archaeology of Love*, specifically in "Dépaysé" and "Samson's Secret". The living garden of Rosroe contrasts with the waste land of "London" and its "dead garden heaped with stone." The happiest poem in the collection is "Living with Animals", which places the woman he loves in a congenial natural setting. Throughout its seven stanzas the landscape of Rosroe and its living creatures form a harmonious context for love. All the actions are expressive of delight—"walking", "diving", "laughing", "circling", "planting". It is an Edenic world in which the notes of danger in the last stanza, in "marauding", are "moving away". At the centre of the idealised portrait is the "you" figure in an act of union and communion with nature:

> Kittiwakes are circling
> Around your head
> As I heard you sing
> Their names to the wood.

In a Murphy poem, happiness is embodied in such acts of understanding relationship with nature: naming and singing are one. To be "perfectly alive" and to have "the happiest of voices" is to be capable of such self-possessed possession. Wittgenstein, too, "shored/His logical weapon" on this "savage promontory". One might also note that the interaction between figure and setting is a dual affair: nature is not passive, but responsive; its

119

creatures are alive and that quality of animation is expressive of as well as conducive to the happiness in the voice of the woman. By being perfectly alive, the creatures complete and embody the Edenic aspects of the place. The "I" figure, also present, enjoys the picture, which he records: "I woke", "I heard". "I watch", "I hear"; it takes place on "my land". The language throughout is simple, direct and formal.

"Girl at the Seaside" has the same clarity and objectivity, but uses words for a surreal effect. Here the visible and the concrete world is not what it seems to be. The inability of the "I" figure to fix reality in its place is symptomatic of her mental state. The stability and security of what is outwardly real fail her:

> I lean on a lighthouse rock
> Where the seagowns flow,
> A trawler slips from the dock
> Sailing years ago.

Whatever solidity may be contained in the opening line is quickly eroded in the movements of the other three, in the ambivalence of seagowns, in the temporal uncertainty that follows, and throughout the stanza in the slender, slipping quality of the " I " sounds. As the poem advances hallucination increases, based on the apparent reliability of real objects—wind, tobacco, seamen—but these form part of the unreal "green air" and the touch of myth in "A head of snakes". The moment of passion turns to misery and there are discordant conjunctions of myth, sensuality, religion and guilt. The apprehensive figure in the last two stanzas grows from these uncertainties and tensions. In the last line she teeters on the inviting, suicidal wish to escape from "talk". Throughout the poem she has combined the habit of analysis and argument with the inability to perceive the actual in clear terms. It is this failure to cope, this failure of reason, that drives her to the "blue cliff-top" in the last stanza where the rhymes of "top" and "stop" were subtly anticipated in the first by "rock" and "dock."

In *Sailing to an Island* (1963), the doomed persona in "The Poet on the Island" "stumbling under the burden of himself" crosses to the island in search of "refuge" and acceptance by the people. Despite the restorative effects of nature, he remains a "stranger" and "lonely". Murphy treats this failure in a sympathetic way, considerate of the craft of the poet, who is seen as a victim: "His fate was like fish under poetry's beaks". In "Woman of the House", from the same collection, she whose life embodies the ordered ways and good deeds of the Big House, ends her days in hospital certified as insane. Her hallucinations have an ironic poignancy:

'The House in flames and nothing is insured!
Send for the doctor, let the horses go.
The dogs are barking again. Has the cow
Calved in the night? What is that great singed bird?

The image of the birds permeates the poetry, in the portraits of Wittgenstein and Roethke as well as "Portrait of a Painter", and throughout the High Island collection.

Murphy does not continue to write portraits of mental breakdown, but he does occasionally portray men in the grip of frightening circumstances and with an impressive use of language. In the following passage Pat Concannon, stunned and blinded by waves, reels in his boat:

The wind began to play, like country fiddlers
In a crowded room, with nailed boots stamping
On the stone cottage floor, raising white ashes.
The sea became a dance. He staggered to the floor
As the music unleashed him, spun in a circle.
Now he was dancing round the siege of Death:
Now he was Death, they were dancing around him,
White robed dancers with crowns and clubs,
With white masked faces, and hands like claws
Flaying his eyes, as they clinched and swung.
He was holding the rope as the dance subsided.

The point is in the last line: Concannon held firm to the line, despite the dance of death in which touches of the barbaric and of ritual press upon him. These have their origin in the familiar image of the country dance but the pattern of those dances, the figures moving in circles round an individual dancer are replaced and distorted in the description of the waves as menacing masked figures, like mummers, but also animalistic. The stanza is charged with the terror and tension of the occasion.

Murphy's poems of the sea, while noted for their objective use of language, have passages in which the transforming power of language is evident. This is particularly noticeable when he wants to indicate the changing rhythms in the pull of the water when these are illuminated through the description itself. Two different kinds of movement may serve to illustrate this skill. The first is again from "The Cleggan Disaster" in a passage that is crucial if one is to understand the authority as well as the courage of Pat Concannon. He is not just grimly holding on, but uses the weight of the nets and the ebb-tide to pull the boat against the wind and away from the dangerous rocks. When he finally cuts the line, the boat has reached calmer water and they can row into the harbour at Inishbofin.

> Down in the deep where the storm could not go
> The ebb-tide, massive and slow, was drawing
> Windwards the ninety-six fathom of nets
> With hundreds of mackerel thickly meshed,
> Safely tugging the boat off the mainland shore.
> The moon couldn't shine, the clouds shut her out,
> But she came unseen to sway on his side
> All the waters gathered from the great spring tide.

The achievement of that kind of language is that it does so much—echoing the massive movement of the deep in its own slow, heaving, top-heavy movement—and at the same time gives the necessary explanation, lifting at the end in affirmation and confirmation of the seaman's mastery and knowledge.

As another example of terror on the sea there is the description of a storm in "Sailing to an Island".

> Now she dips, and the sail hits the water.
> She luffs to a squall; is struck; and shudders.
> Someone is shouting. The boom, weak as a scissors,
> Has snapped. The boatman is praying.
> Orders thunder and canvas cannonades.
> She smothers in spray.

The confusion of sounds and movements echo through the lines in which the interrupted and fragmentary syntax illuminates as well as describes. The sounds hiss and spit; the basic four stress lines halt and plunge, the sickening fall of the boat is mimicked in the separation of stressed syllables—she *luffs* to a *squall*—or holds blindly under the dousing of sounds—she *smothers in spray*. The aural quality of much of this poetry of the sea is everywhere evident in these lines, as is the sense of drama. The poem is a voyage of initiation which involves the purging of foolish dreams in the reality of the sea; the kind of wisdom Concannon embodies has yet to be learned.

There is an elemental quality in many of Murphy's poems of the sea; their kinship with Anglo-Saxon voyages, contests, laments, seascapes and hazards is not merely a matter of four stressed lines as in "The Last Galway Hooker". The sea is a pleasure ground because it can bring the exhilaration of freedom, the testing of the self, and then the imaginative recovery of such experience in words. "I'll tell the truth" the narrator says in "Pat Cloherty's Version of *The Maisie*" and he does so, succinctly, clearly, unemotionally but with such fidelity, and such a persuasive use of oral techniques, that the impact is direct.

The poems of the sea are not reflections of one another; each has its revealing tonal textures, characteristic rhythms and states of feeling. The qualities described in the above extracts are quite different from those in "The Last Galway Hooker" in which the respect for skill and craft, and the respect for the boat herself, are present in the concluding lines. The notes of satisfaction result from the feeling of a job well done: the ship's blood-line, as it were her pedigree has been proven, her history recounted and accepted, and now the skilled men assemble.

> Her skilful sailmaker,
> Her inherited boatwright, her dream-tacking steersman
> Picked up the tools of their interrupted work,
>
> And in memory's hands this hooker was restored.
> Old men my instructors, and with all new gear
> May I handle her well down tomorrow's sea-road.

The link with the early poem "Auction" is clear, but sounded with more confidence and relish. We may hear an echo of Yeats and his ghostly instructors, or more remotely of Stephen Dedalus packing his gear for Europe. What we notice unmistakeably is the joyful anticipation of the man taking on his role—in the company of craftsmen. It might be said that the manner works against the situation, being too cold, too documentary, too limited by a strict denotative use of words—*sailmaker, boatright, steersman*— but these are proud terms that in Murphy's view need no further embellishment.

When we look for connotative uses of language, we find traces in *The Battle of Aughrim* (1969), in lyric sections about the

Rapparees blending and fusing with the landscape, in the plaintive account of the wolfhound guarding the body of the dead ensign, in the historical evocation of "the wild geese have flown", in the resonance of "choirs are silenced in wood and stone", or in the paradox and antithesis of the first stanza of the section on Roger Casement:

> After the noose, and the black diary deeds
> Gossiped, his fame roots in prison lime:
> The hanged bones burn, a revolution seeds.
> Now Casement's skeleton is flying home.

This language is quick with the paradox of life in death: despite the noose and the shame, his fame "roots"; bones burn with quicklime but also with reputation, and so on. The alert consciousness in this section relates directly to the artifacts of the past: the act of resurrection expressed through the image of Casement's skeleton flying home is raised to an act of faith in the transmuting power of the imagination. Murphy in this poem, as well as in his poems about ancestors and his lyrics about High Island, is the archaeolgoist of the imagination, a notion of poetry already present in the title of his first book. The uses of the classical past there foreshadowed the uses of the Irish past in this long historical meditation.

> Touch unearths military history.
> Sifting clay on a mound, I find
> Bones and bullets fingering my mind:
> The past is happening today.

"The battle cause", he says "has a beginning in my blood."
The activity, one notes, is a two way relationship, on the one side the responsiveness of the poet, on the other the far from dead matter of the past. The "happening" is a result of this interaction of forces. The "beginning" is in his blood—in the sense of heritage, since his ancestors, and those of most Irish families, were on both sides in this important battle; he takes his beginning from this battle, since it shaped his destiny in the sense of class and religion; a beginning also in the now of the poem, in the poet's awakened response, beginning in the word. In this conclusion we get an answer to the opening question:

Who owns the land where musket-balls are buried
In blackthorn roots on the eskar, the drained bogs
Where sheep browse, and credal war miscarried?
Names in the rival churches are written on plaques.

That question raises a number of issues about landownership, about imaginative possession, about actual ownership now, and about the way in which a contemporary landscape yields up a reading of the past. But the last line connects with the army roll list in the last section in which ownership becomes a poetic right, by virtue of the imagination's power to respond and to reactivate and to apprehend. One answer to the question—who owns the landscape?—is, the poet. Throughout the whole first section he has revealed his power of dual perception, the contemporary scene and within it and on equal terms with it—the past. Thus in stanza two what does he see behind the dog-rose ditch? The modern tractor, but also the pikes. The morning fog lifts to reveal summer hikers, and for him the morning of the battle which was also foggy. The hikers go to bathe in a stream, but a stream passed by cavalry traitors. That overlapping, dual vision, determines the method of the poem, which is less a narrative than a series of individual vignettes that mirror each other to a variety of effects.

Throughout *The Battle of Aughrim* we find equations of opposites, in the political, sectarian, and social areas, that play with and against each other through the poem's several voices, which in themselves are distinctive accents of race and class. The poem works through major contrasts and parallels in its four Parts, and through similar patterns between sections and within particular sections. These correspondences even extend outside the poem through the explicit connection with the divisions in Northern Ireland that erupted once again as Murphy was completing his poem, and through the implicit analogy with the contemporary feud of absent powers in Vietnam.

Richard Murphy's response to words, to their sound, meaning, etymology, and texture, is particularly noticeable in *High Island* (1974). In "Nocturne", almost an exercise in onomatopeia, the cries and signals of the petrels are echoed in the sounds and stresses: "Wings beating on stone; Quick vibrations of notes throats tongues." In "Stormpetrel" he plays with words to suggest the quick movements of the birds and brings in archaic, dialect and colloquial terms—"wambling", "jooking", "jink". In each stanza, the metaphor invoked in the opening word is carried forward to the last line, as in stanza two:

> Guest of the storm
> Who sweeps you off to party after party,
> You flit in a sooty grey coat
> Smelling of must
> Barefoot across a sea of broken glass.

The opening word of each stanza invokes the bird as "gypsy", "guest", "waif" and "pulse"; the last, an endearment from the Irish, brings the poem to a tender conclusion. All the verbs in the poem convey the movements of the bird, as do the four terms of apostrophe. "Seals at High Island" is rich with the movement of tide and mammal: "Swayed by the thrust and backfall of the tide."

A number of poems—"The Writing Lesson", "The Reading Lesson", and "Coppersmith"—call attention to the problems of language, the difficulties of expression, the relationship between language and identity. "What are words made of? Squiggles, lines, dots." That is the child's view. In the parallel poem in which that child, grown up, understands how alien the task of learning to read is to the tinker, his bafflement is sympathetically rendered:

> If books resembled roads, he'd quickly read.
> But they're small farms to him, fenced by the page,
> Ploughed into lines, with letters drilled like oats
> A field of tasks he'll always be outside.

The contrasting dictions in this poem reinforces the differences between teacher and pupil, the civilised and the wild. In mythic terms the poem tries to resolve the friction between Apollo and Hermes. "Coppersmith" recreates the horror of a child's lost identity, when the sound gets separated from the meaning in words, when one cannot exercise the powers of analysis and discrimination:

> The compound spinning round,
> My brain melting, as if I'd stood in the sun
> Too long without a topee and was going blind,
> Till I and the bird, the word and the tree, were one.

There are echoes of Pat Concannon reeling in his boat and of the girl at the seaside ready to "drop through the sea-air/Till everything stops". The poems of Ceylon render the recoil from an alien culture, from customs, smells, voices, religions that the boy cannot accept. That experience is the antithesis of the one in "The Reading Lesson". In one the boy is isolated within the world of class and privilege, in the other the boy cannot fit in to Irish society. The difference lies in the nature of the adult response: in Ceylon the adult figure is remote, distasteful—"A lion rampant on a little hairy finger"; in Ireland the adult understands the boy's attitude. Murphy's imaginative sympathies include both and the two poems substantiate the view of him as a poet of two traditions. To the untameable wildness of the Irish tradition he brings his inherent urge to impose order. The concept of the wild garden that must be pruned and civilised is central to English literary tradition and the orderliness of Murphy's work attests his loyalty to his Anglo-Irish background. The world of the pleasure ground, the avenue of lime trees, the sense of tradition, survives in the ordered lines and the civilised procedures of his work. But he knows the risks. When you tame wild creatures, as the poem "Care" (p. 32) points out, you make them vulnerable. Wildness itself is a virtue and should be respected and this principle animates the poetry of High Island. "Stormpetrel", for example, in its careful selection of words and in its rapidity of movement is a tribute to the untamed life of the bird. Throughout the book there is this inherent respect for the world of nature—the seals, the corncrake, the petrels—their freedom and grace, which the poet records and with which he animates his chosen landscape.

It follows naturally from this attitude that the central figure in these poems is more of an observer than a participant: he watches the holy mating of the seals, he leans above the assembly of birds, he watches the ceremonies in Ceylon, he notes how the archaeologists give new life to old stone, he is separate from the couple in "Sunup". Another feature of the book is the violence of event, reduced in these condensed narratives to as restricted a space as possible: murder, drowning, sexual violence, fighting, destruction, robbery, deceit, betrayal, nightmare and panic. At the same time, despite the sense of the persona as solitary, some poems are recognitions and celebrations of community, integration, and the renewals of history. The island itself is haven and marker, womb and phallus. The region, not idealised as was Rosroe in "Living with Animals", is a world in which the persona walks and talks, whose landmarks he has made his own in these acts of imaginative possession. It is a poetry of metaphor, simile, and onomatopoeia, of connotative power, expressive of personal feeling, with touches of the mystical fusion and interchange of the animate and the inaminate. It is too a poetry of varying rhythms, the syntax sometimes loose, the metres sometimes strict; it is formal in diction but at times colloquial, a poetry that makes claims upon this world, but that also respects its autonomy. Beginning with words, Murphy in this latest collection, shows a greater awareness and mastery of the possibilities of words than ever before. Rooting himself long ago in the landscape of the west, he is now gathering his harvest with patience and care.